WOOD-FIRED COOKING

# WOOD-FIRED COOKING

## TECHNIQUES AND RECIPES FOR THE GRILL, BACKYARD OVEN, FIREPLACE, AND CAMPFIRE

Mary Karlin

Photography by Ed Anderson

TEN SPEED PRESS
Berkeley | Toronto

Ten Speed Press
PO Box 7123
Berkeley, California 94707
www.tenspeed.com

Distributed in Australia by Simon and Schuster Australia, in Canada by Ten Speed Press Canada, in New Zealand by Southern Publishers Group, in South Africa by Real Books, and in the United Kingdom and Europe by Publishers Group UK.

Cover and text design by Nancy Austin
Food and prop styling by Jenny Martin-Wong

The Aztec Grill, Beehive Oven, Big Green Egg, La Caja China, and SoJoe Fire Pit are registered trademarks. Used by permission.

Library of Congress Cataloging-in-Publication Data
Karlin, Mary.
  Wood-fired cooking : techniques and recipes for the grill, backyard oven, fireplace, and campfire / Mary Karlin ; photography by  Ed Anderson.
      p. cm.
  Includes index.
  Summary: "A collection of 100 contemporary recipes for the range of wood-fired cooking options, including globally inspired Indian, Mediterranean, Italian, American, and North African recipes for cooking over live flame and embers"
—Provided by publisher.
  ISBN 978-1-58008-945-6
  1.  Barbecue cookery. 2.  Cookery, International.  I. Title.
  TX840.B3K3656 2009
  641.7′6—dc22

                    2008041621

Printed in China
First printing, 2009
1 2 3 4 5 6 7 8 9 10 — 13 12 11 10 09

# CONTENTS

# FOREWORD

Cooking with fire kindles an ancient and primal memory in human beings. According to anthropologists, fire provided the spark for modern human evolution, but not because it allowed our ancestors to eat meat. Rather, it was the ability to cook hard roots like carrots, potatoes, and beets that caused hominids to turn an important evolutionary corner almost 2 million years ago. Not only did we change physically (among other developments, our teeth became smaller, since cooked food was easier to eat), but fire was the genesis for creating flavors that we didn't know existed when only raw food was consumed. Once this wider range of tastes was discovered, our innate curiosity and desire for more and different taste experiences set about an exploration that continues to this day. Who we are then is in large measure a result of our learning to cook our food.

The ingenious ways that humans have adapted fire for cooking are amazing. From cooking food impaled on a stick or fixed to a plank over a campfire, to the creation of various types of earthen ovens, to today's high-tech stainless steel grills, there is a technique for everyone and every budget.

Almost everyone has a fond memory of cooking over fire, even if it was just s'mores on a camping trip. I remember the fishing trips with my grandparents in Colorado. We'd go out for three or four days at a time, camping near streams and "cricks" and fishing all day for native trout. We brought little else with us, just coffee to wake us up in the morning, cornmeal to dust the fresh fish with, and bacon fat to cook them in. The tool of choice was a Dutch oven with feet that allowed you to set it right in the hot coals: simple but very effective. And once the fish were done, we could scour out the same pot and use it to make a grunt with wild berries. I'll never forget how wonderful that food tasted.

I've had the chance to watch Mary's "cooking with fire" evolution over the years as she experimented with every fire tool and technique she could find. As she developed her skills, she began to teach, and her enthusiastic students begat a whole new generation of fire aficionados. I was pleased to share part of that journey with her.

Cooking with fire has a magical and powerful ability to connect us to each other. Kudos to Mary for giving us all a taste of the delicious possibilities of wood-fired cooking.

—John Ash

**To all of the fired-up bakers, chefs, and everyday cooks who make and share extraordinary wood-fired food.**

## Acknowledgments

Thank you to Northern California's numerous talented bakers, cooks, chefs, farmers, and artisan food purveyors for sharing your passions and influencing my style of cooking and living. A special thanks to Alice Waters and Joyce Goldstein inspiring me with their authenticity and heart for cooking and sharing simple, good food.

I thank Allan Scott, the endearing guru of wood-fired brick ovens, for getting me hooked on fire and sparking my quest for an oven. Heart-filled thanks to my best friend, Bert Archer, who found his inner baker by building my brick oven and pushed me to write this book.

A giant thanks to my family at Ramekins Cooking School for their love and support; thank you for introducing me to many talented culinary educators and for helping me to find my teaching voice. A big hug of thanks to Suzanne Brangham who unknowingly jump-started this book.

My infinite gratitude to Peter Reinhart for his ever present guidance and generosity. A toast to the guest contributors: Bruce Aidells, John Ash, Georgeanne Brennan, Linda Carucci, Tim Decker, Fran Gage, Cheryl and Bill Jamison, Deborah Madison, John McReynolds, Peter Reinhart, Tom Romano, Jerry Traunfeld, Joanne Weir and Paula Wolfert. I am honored you are part of this.

I am eternally grateful for the generosity of these manufacturers who shared their knowledge and products: Aztec Grill, Big Green Egg, Forno Bravo, La Caja China, NapaStyle, Pacific Coast Brick Ovens, SoJoe Fire Pits, SpitJack, and Wood Stone Ovens.

A special thank you to my team of recipe testers: Kay Austin, Suzy Foster, Nancy Lang, Lisa Lavagetto, Stephen McBurney, Sally McComas, John McReynolds, Annie Simmons, and Eileen Tyson. Good job! An added hug to Kay, Sally, and Annie for assisting me at the photo shoot.

A special nod of gratitude to Aaron Wehner and Lorena Jones at Ten Speed for embracing this topic and having faith in my vision. Thank you to my editor, Melissa Moore, for her thoughtful suggestions, skillful organizational eye, and unwavering enthusiasm. Applause to the blazing creative team: Ed Anderson, photographer extraordinaire; Jenny Martin-Wong, talented stylist; and Nancy Austin, keen designer.

Other nods of thanks to: Dianne Jacob for being a great coach and helping me develop my writing voice; Georgeanne Brennan and Diane Phillips for being my big sisters; Paula Wolfert being my mentor; John Ash for sharing the journey; Toni Allegra for supporting my teaching vision; Kathleen Hill and Sally Bernstein for encouraging my writing; Sue Simon, James Cribb, and Sonoma Dog Camp for caring for Ginger; Priscilla Hoback for sharing her horno, friends, and great food; Ann Funsten for allowing me to build my oven; the special friends who gather with me at the fire; and my students, who continue to explore and share their wood-fired experiences.

Now, slow down and smell the smoke.

# INTRODUCTION

Welcome to the amazing world of wood-fired cooking. Whether you are new to this form of cooking, just curious, or are already a devotee stoking fires regularly for the pleasure of family and friends, this book was created for you.

*Wood-Fired Cooking* will take you on a comprehensive journey of wood-fired cooking in all its contemporary forms. It includes more than one hundred flavor-packed recipes, plus fireside stories and cooking tips. Some of the best-known authors and cooks on wood-fired cooking have joined me to cook and create some recipes for this book.

Wood-fired cooking, the foundation of a wide variety of cuisines from all over the world, includes a variety of techniques, from grilling, baking, and roasting to braising, barbecuing, and smoking. *Barbecue, kebab, satay, pizza, tandoori, rotisserie* are all words describing traditional wood-fired foods and techniques that have become part of our contemporary cuisine. The wide variety of wood-fired cooking methods makes the creation of delicious globally inspired food easy and fun.

While it's wonderful to have your own backyard oven or ceramic cooker, you don't really need a special cooking appliance to use this book. Most wood-fired dishes, with the exception of loaf breads, can be cooked on a wood-fired grill (flatbreads, however, are easily cooked on a grill), or in a conventional oven—though you will lose out on the smoky flavor that wood-fired cooking imparts.

All of the recipes in this book are drawn from cuisines that have brought wood-fired cooking to a high art. Many of them are steeped with the spirit of the Mediterranean—the tastes, aromas, and colors of the region, its lifestyle, and its food. Cuisines from other lands of the sun, especially Morocco and India, are also found here, transformed, like the others, by the California emphasis on freshness and innovation.

Each of the most popular wood-fired methods is thoroughly covered in this book: grilling, baking, and roasting, smoking, barbecuing, fire-pit and campfire cooking. As the popularity of live-fire cooking continues to grow throughout America, more and more wood-fired cookers, appliances, and devices have become available. This book tells you how to use all of them.

After a brief chapter on the history of wood-fired cooking, the basics of cooking with wood are discussed—everything you need to know to prepare the more than one hundred recipes that have been specifically developed to form the heart of this book. You'll learn how to prepare wonderfully flavored rustic foods for your family and friends in a tradition that goes back to the beginning of cooking with fire.

Now, let's start our fiery adventure!

# CHAPTER 1

# Cooking with Fire

Cooking with fire was one of the first steps humans took on the road toward civilization. Lightning fires and erupting volcanoes were man's first experiences with fire, and the accidental burning of animal carcasses undoubtedly introduced cooked meat to humans for the first time. But eventually fire was tamed enough to be used for open-fire and pit cooking, the oldest methods of cooking with fire.

### Open-Fire Cooking: The First Grills

On the plains, in mountain caves, and around the campfire—whether on a spit or a metal grid suspended on a circle of rocks—open-fire cooking is a tradition that crosses all cultural and ethnic boundaries and is deeply infused in current culture.

Anthropologists tell us that man has been cooking over open fires since the Stone Age, making it the oldest and most widespread form of cooking. Developed by nomadic hunter-gatherers, open-fire cooking preceded contained-heat cooking in wood-fired ovens because it required only suspending part of an animal carcass over an open fire or burying it in live coals.

Eventually, techniques of cooking in animal skins, then pottery, allowed humans to boil and bake foods suspended over an open fire. But the discovery of metallurgy advanced open-fire cooking exponentially with the development of bronze cooking vessels and implements, including spears that did double duty as spits and skewers.

The first grill grates were no doubt simply green saplings crossed over a fire at right angles. When the Spanish landed in the Caribbean, they discovered the native population cooking food over an open fire on a grate woven of green sticks; the Indian word for this grate entered the Spanish language as *barbacoa*. Native Americans also attached fish to slabs of wood propped up at the edge of an open fire, a technique now known as planking.

The development of the home fireplace brought open-fire cooking indoors, where food was suspended over the fire on spits or in metal pots hung from hooks. Food was also cooked directly in the coals or at the edge of the fire, or on metal grates with legs set in the coals. Today, the Tuscan grill, a wrought-iron implement that fits into a fireplace opening, allows wood-fire enthusiasts to grill in their own living room throughout the year.

In this country, the *barbacoa* evolved over the years into the barbecue grill, becoming popular in the 1920s, when Henry Ford produced the first charcoal briquettes from scrap wood left over from making Model T's. Until the 1940s, grilling in America mostly took place at campsites or picnics. As the middle class began moving from the cities to the suburbs after World War II, backyard grilling took hold, becoming all the rage by the 1950s. Grilling's newfound popularity was due in great part to the invention of the Weber kettle grill in 1951 by George Stephen, a metal worker at Weber Brothers Metal Spinning Company, a company best known as a maker of harbor buoys. Stephen was frustrated with the flat, open grills that were popular at the time and was supposedly inspired to cut a harbor buoy in half, adding a grate and using the top as a lid. He added some vents for controlling the temperature, and the Weber kettle grill was born. Backyard grilling has never been the same. The Weber kettle grill is still popular and has spawned numerous new versions. Variations on it range from halved steel drums for huge cookouts, to disk-shaped fire pits, to massive mesquite-fired grills the size of a restaurant stove.

## Underground Earthen Pits: The First Ovens

Fire pits were the first ovens: Cavities dug into the ground were lined with rocks, and a fire was built in the pit to heat the rocks. Once the coals burned down and the rocks were hot, the food was placed inside and covered during cooking. Fire pits are still popular today, especially in the tropics where the ground can be dug year-round.

Food cooked in pits is typically wrapped in plant leaves such as banana or maguey if the portions of food are small; if a whole animal carcass is being cooked a layer of vegetation is placed over the carcass for both protection and flavor. The covered food is then topped with a layer of dirt, then rocks to keep the cavity secure. This subterranean steam- and smoke-fed "oven" allows long, slow cooking with succulent results, thanks to the moist environment. Pit cooking remains popular around the world. In this country, its best-known version is the clambake, a legacy of the Native Americans, but the dug out campfires of the American West's cowboys and vaqueros also descended from fire pits. Today's box roasters are based on the principles of fire-pit cooking, and produce consistently succulent roasted foods.

## Chamber Ovens:
## Vertical, Dome, and Egg-Shaped

Wood-fired chamber ovens have either rounded or squared compartments for cooking and are of two basic shapes: either vertical, like the tandoor oven, or horizontal, like the dome-shaped oven, sometimes called a Roman oven due to its existence dating back to the days of Pompeii. In both cases, the heat required for baking or roasting has been generated and stored in the structural mass of the vessel before cooking takes place. Sometimes a small fire is kept burning in the oven to maintain even heat. A door (or lid, in the case of a tandoor) is placed into the oven opening during cooking to keep the generated heat and smoke in the chamber.

The first wood-fired chamber ovens were probably built thousands of years ago in Egypt. We know that the peoples of the southern and eastern Mediterranean cultivated grain and ground it into flour to make simple unleavened flatbreads, which were cooked on a flat stone surrounded and fueled by smaller fire-heated stones. As leavened breads were developed, the first chamber ovens were crafted: vertical ovens molded from clay to yield the kind of sustained, even heat needed to bake yeasted doughs. Traditionally made of local clay, vertical ovens have their heat source in their base, and versions of them are found in native cultures around the world. The best known to Westerners is the Indian tandoor, which uses a coal or wood fire. Flatbread dough is slapped onto the walls of the heated cylinder to quickly bake, and seasoned meats and vegetables are suspended on metal skewers and placed in the heated cavity, where they cook from the radiant heat of the masonry walls and the small fire at the base. These ovens were traditionally buried in the ground, and the cook would sit on the ground to cook the food.

Today's egg-shaped ovens are directly descended from the vertical clay oven. One of the best known is the *kamado*. Developed over three thousand years ago in China, this charcoal-fired clay cooker was adopted by the Japanese, who gave it its name, which means "oven" or "fireplace." These cookers have an egg-shaped, insulated ceramic body with a grill grate that is near the top of the body, making them a combination of grill and oven: When the lid is off, they function just as a grill; with the lid on, they retain heat comparable to an oven. And, when heated to low temperatures, they are also effective smokers. After World War II, thousands of American soldiers brought these cookers home to the United States just as the grilling craze was on the rise. Today's versions of these cookers have evolved in styling and efficiency and are extremely versatile.

Early European dome ovens were large versions of the horizontal Roman oven and made of regional clay and stones. They were built to bake large quantities of bread and were located in the center of the village, where they functioned as a communal oven and a gathering place. Most villages had large dome ovens that were managed by the village bakers. Once the daily bread had been baked, the villagers were allowed to use the still-hot ovens to cook dishes of food for themselves. These communal ovens stayed in use in Europe until after World War II, when home ovens began to become available.

The wood-fired pizza oven in a variety of shapes is one modern version of the dome oven, which has become newly popular today. Some homeowners build their own traditional clay or masonry ovens, while several companies offer plans for permanent bread ovens, and others sell portable versions.

# CHAPTER 2

# Wood-Fired Basics

Whether known as a *forno,* an *horno,* a tandoor, a *churrasco,* a *kamado,* or a hibachi, wood-fired ovens and grills have been used for cooking for thousands of years in all cultures.

Thanks to modern technology, the options for wood-fired cooking have increased dramatically in recent years, and the efficiency of wood-fired appliances has also increased significantly. Today's wood-fire cook has a veritable treasure trove of indoor and outdoor cooker options to choose from: Tuscan grills and pizza ovens, cowboy campfire fire pits, smokers, egg-shaped cookers, and box roasters, all ranging from the most basic to the highly sophisticated.

## Getting Started

Following is general advice on choosing an appliance, selecting fuel, starting and maintaining a fire, and cookware options.

### Choosing a Wood-Fired Appliance

Whether you choose a wood-fired oven, grill, or cooker, efficiency should be a key consideration. The better the appliance's materials, insulation, heat retention, and radiant heat, the more efficiently it will function. It's also important to consider the

Clockwise, from top left: SoJoe Fire Pit, Beehive Oven, Big Green Egg, and small La Caja China box roaster.

type of fuel you'll use in the appliance and the efficiency of that fuel.

Cooking on an open grill with thin metal walls and without insulation means valuable heat is lost to the atmosphere—making it more likely that you'll need to keep adding fuel during the course of cooking. However, with a dome oven that's well insulated with heavy metal, brick, clay, or ceramic housing, you'll have phenomenal retained and radiant heat, which means less fuel consumption overall and better cooking results.

Choose wood-fired cooking appliances based on their cooking properties and your cooking style. Here's an overview of wood-fired appliance options, from the simplest (and most economical) to most elaborate:

• Campfire or underground pit
• Indoor or outdoor fireplace
• Tuscan grill in fireplace or on campfire
• Vessel fire pit
• Box roaster
• Florentine grill
• Big Green Egg
• Beehive portable oven
• Aztec wood-burning grill
• Portable refractory wood-fired oven
• Refractory pizza oven
• Built-in ceramic, soapstone, or masonry oven

## Choosing Responsible Fuel for Cooking

To do our part to protect our environment, we need to make informed decisions and ethical purchases, especially when it comes to the energy and resources we use to cook. The heat produced by

## Wood-Fired Cooking

| WOOD-FIRED ENVIRONMENT | TYPE OF HEAT |
|---|---|
| Open fire | Direct and indirect heat; quick or extended cooking |
| Three-sided chamber with flue | Direct and indirect heat; quick or extended cooking; roasting and grilling |
| Vertical clay top-vented oven | Direct, indirect, and convection heat; residual heat for extended cooking |
| Horizontal masonry, clay, or stone oven | |
| Underground, covered chamber | Indirect heat; low and slow cooking |
| Top-heated horizontal chamber | |
| Bottom- and top-fueled ceramic cooker | Direct and indirect heat |
| Vertical or horizontal enclosed chamber | Indirect heat; low and slow cooking |

# Environments and Appliance Characteristics

| FOOD TO COOK | GENERIC DEVICES | DESCRIPTION | BRAND EXAMPLES | APPROXIMATE TIME TO HEAT TO 400°F |
|---|---|---|---|---|
| Spit-roasted meats and poultry, over-coals grilling, in-ember roasting | Campfire | Simple ring of rocks or bricks to contain fire; with grill or spit rotisserie | | 30 minutes |
| | Cowboy grill; Tuscan grill | Tripod or grate over live fire | Cowboy Campfire Grill | 30 minutes |
| | Vessel fire pit | Open grill or with spit rotisserie | SoJoe | 30 minutes |
| | Tabletop charcoal grill | Small cast-iron grill with a shallow charcoal pan and grate | Japanese hibachi | 15 minutes |
| | Kettle, drum, or box roaster grill; open grate grill | Deep, metal charcoal pan with grid and vents, with a grate suspended above and lid to close | Weber Kettle, Char-Broil, Ace, Masterbuilt, Aztec Grill, Florentine grill | 40 minutes to 45 minutes |
| Pizza and flatbreads, steaks and ribs, chicken, skewered meats and vegetables, grilled fruits, spit-roasted meats and poultry | Fireplace (home or campground) | Hearth, grate grill, or spit rotisserie over live fire | | 30 minutes |
| Hearth breads; pizzas and flatbreads; hearth grilled, roasted, or braised meats and vegetables; baked desserts | Tandoor | Bottom-fueled, recessed, insulated clay cylinder with open top or vented | Wood Stone Tandoor, Big Green Egg | 30 minutes |
| | Dome oven; refractory pizza oven; horno | Domed shape with door, front flue | Wood Stone oven, Beehive Oven, Forno Bravo, Mugnaini | 45 minutes to 2 hours, depending on brand |
| Barbecued and slow-roasted meats, poultry, fish, and vegetables | Pit: Barbacoa, Hawaiian Umi, American Clambake | Cavity in ground lined with rocks, covered with dirt or metal lid | | 1 hour |
| | Box roaster | Metal-lined box with top heat | La Caja China | Never reaches over 300°F |
| | Kamado | Egg-shaped charcoal cooker and smoker | Big Green Egg | 30 minutes |
| Smoked meat, poultry, fish, cheese, and assorted pantry items | Smoker | Brick, stainless steel, or ceramic chamber for capturing smoke and heat for cooking | Pitts & Spitts, Landmann QuadQue, Horizon BBQ Smoker | Uses temperatures under 250°F |

burning wood or the wood by-product lump charcoal, also known as charwood, is actually the energy of the sun (solar energy), which the trees store as chemical energy. Unlike fossil fuels or fuel products that contain petroleum products (such as briquettes containing fillers), firewood releases no more harmful greenhouse gases than would be produced if the wood were to simply decompose on the forest floor. As a renewable, biomass fuel, firewood is abundant and inexpensive compared to burning fossil fuels.

The cleanest-burning woods are seasoned (dried) hardwoods and fruitwoods, because they are dense and low in sap and resin, unlike softwoods such as pine. Look for local sources of these woods, ideally with logs of about the same length and diameter to ensure even heat. Oak, maple, ash, and walnut are some of the best choices, plus any fruitwood (find out more at www.consciousconsuming.com, www.hpba .org, or www.nakedwhiz.com/lump.htm).

Other clean-burning options are certain brands of densified, or pressurized, all-wood fire logs and lump charcoal, which is charred natural wood (see Resources). Also, look for sawmill slabs of untreated lumber, an inexpensive and ecological waste product from a local industry.

### A RESPONSIBLE FIRE ENVIRONMENT

In order for wood to burn completely and efficiently, you must create an environment that includes a proper mix of fuel, oxygen, and heat. Practice *responsible fuel-burning* and minimize fire emissions by using seasoned hardwood and burning small, hot fires. Charwood is the product of incomplete combustion of hardwood and is primarily carbon; it is 20 to 25 percent of the original volume of the wood, and when it burns it doesn't produce as much smoke as burning wood and will burn long, hot, and steady. Lump charcoal yields a larger amount of heat in proportion to its volume than a corresponding quantity of fresh wood, and also produces less ash than processed charcoal.

Use seasoned hardwood that has been dried for at least 6 months, and preferably up to 2 years; it should have a moisture content of 20 percent or less. Wood with greater moisture creates more smoke in the combustion process, which is essentially unburned fuel. Also, because a fire's smoke and soot are particulate matter that will go into the atmosphere, it's important to keep smoke emissions as low as possible. The combustion temperature is partly determined by the specific variety of wood and its moisture content. (See the Cooking Hardwoods and Fruitwoods chart opposite for more detailed information.)

## Making a Kettle Grill Efficient

Due to their thin metal walls, kettle grills such as the ubiquitous Weber grill are very inefficient for cooking that requires anything more than a short time over high heat. But it's very easy to improve the efficiency of these grills by giving them a bit of insulation by adding fire bricks to the floor and walls of the grill.

## Hardwoods and Fruitwoods

Wood for cooking is judged by four different factors: flavor profile, uses, heat level, and coaling quality. The flavor profile refers to the flavor that each type of wood imparts to food during the cooking process, while the uses highlights the best cooking applications for each. The heat level describes how hot the different types of wood burn, and the coaling quality means the ability of wood to form a long-lasting bed of hot coals when burned (which equates to fuel efficiency). This chart describes the most popular woods used for cooking. Other fruitwoods, such as chestnut, fig, olive, peach, pear, plum, and apricot, are also used for cooking. All add a sweet flavor and fragrance to food.

## Cooking Hardwoods and Fruitwoods Chart

| WOOD | FLAVOR PROFILE | USES | HEAT LEVEL | COALING QUALITY |
|---|---|---|---|---|
| Alder | Delicate with hint of smoky-sweet | Fish and vegetables, pork, poultry and light-meat game | Medium-low | Good |
| Almond | Nutty and sweet | All meats | Low | Good |
| Apple | Slightly fruity | Beef, poultry, game birds, pork | High-medium | Great |
| Ash | Sublte flavor | Fish and red meat | High | Good to great |
| Cherry | Slightly sweet | All meats, desserts | Medium | Great |
| Citrus | Fruity | Beef, pork, poultry | Medium | Good |
| Hickory* | Pungent, most common | All meats, especially pork | Very high | Great |
| Lilac | Very light and floral | Seafood and lamb | Medium | Good |
| Maple | Mildly smoky and sweet | Pork, poultry, vegetables, game birds | High-medium | Great |
| Mesquite* | Strong and earthy | Most meats, especially beef | Very high | Great |
| Pecan | Less strong than hickory, nutty | Poultry, game birds, pork | High | Good |
| Red oak* | Honey, earthy | Beef and fish | High | Great |
| Walnut | Heavy flavor, usually mixed | Red meats and game | High-medium | Good |
| White oak* | One of most popular | Red meats, pork, fish, game | Very high | Great |

*Also available as lump charcoal.
Adapted from www.barbecuewood.com.

Lower your particulate matter impact by choosing lump charcoal that has been harvested from sustainably managed forests or from invasive tree species in need of clearing. It's also important to check that the charcoal was kiln-processed in a low-oxygen environment that did not use fossil fuels or emit volatile gases.

A side benefit to using lump charcoal is that the cold ash can be recycled into garden compost.

To start your fire responsibly, use kindling made from the same woods you are burning, dried cuttings or small branches from your property, or choose safe, quick starters made from compressed sawdust and paraffin (see Resources). These starters are easily ignited using one match, and produce a nontoxic flame, unlike charcoal lighter fluid, which is toxic. They will light more easily and emit less smoke in the process, keeping your fire efficient. You can also wad up a brown paper bag, douse it with vegetable oil, place kindling or charcoal on top, then light. Always use lump charcoal, which is carbonized wood, not basic charcoal briquettes, which contain fillers and chemicals. Natural briquettes made from natural charcoal are perfectly fine as well.

### Essential Wood-Fired Cooking Tools

In order to properly cook over a live fire, certain tools are essential to your success and safety. Here's my list of must-haves as the foundation to your wood-fired cooking tool chest. You may already have many in your kitchen; a few others are specific to fire tending.

- 6 to 8 stainless steel short and long-reach locking tongs
- Long-handled grilling spatulas and roasting forks
- 8 to 10 heavy-gauge baking sheets

- 4 to 6 silicone basting brushes
- Olive oil mister bottle
- 2 water mister bottles for dousing fire flare-ups
- 2 to 3 wood pizza peels
- Long-reach bubble popper (a hooked tool for popping pizza bubbles), for grabbing the handles of hot pots
- Metal ash bucket
- Ash scoop
- Hearth brush
- Hearth shovel
- Hearth hoe
- Steel poker
- 2 charcoal starter chimneys
- Fire extinguisher
- 5-gallon water bucket
- Laser, probe, oven, and instant-read thermometers
- 2 to 3 pairs heat-resistant, long grilling gloves
- Heavy-quality insulated pot holders
- A dozen or so terry bar towels

### Choosing Cookware

Cookware for wood-fired dishes should be heavy duty and ovenproof. Your best choices are cast iron, either seasoned or enameled, and high-fired glazed terra-cotta or unglazed micaceous clay (see Resources). Other good cookware for wood-fired cooking is heavy stainless steel and anodized aluminum, both great heat conductors. Although copper is a great heat conductor, it doesn't work as well as clay or steel in wood-fired cooking because it gets too hot for most purposes. Unglazed or partially glazed (with glazed walls and unglazed base) clay is more fragile;

it will need tempering for use in a wood-fired oven, and cannot be used over direct heat. Restaurant-quality (heavy-gauge) aluminum baking sheets may be used in wood-fired ovens, and wooden planks can be used for both roasting and grilling.

Here is a list of the different kinds of pans and other cookware most often used for wood-fired cooking (see Resources for more detailed recommendations).

- Dutch ovens, saucepans, and griddles, either cast iron or enameled cast iron
- Cast-iron Potjie "spyder" skillet: Originally from the Netherlands, this is a combination skillet and Dutch oven that is great as a fireplace or campfire cooking utensil. The lid is designed to hold embers to create the top heat essential to some cooking techniques. The three legs are long enough to sit over hot coals and the extra-long handle makes it easy to remove from the fire.
- Skillets in various sizes, either cast iron, heavy stainless steel, anodized aluminum, or enameled cast iron
- Unglazed terra-cotta tagine
- Casserole dishes and gratin dishes, either enameled cast iron or high-fired glazed terra-cotta
- Carbon steel wok
- Carbon steel paella pan
- Unglazed micaceous clay pots: These pit-fired pots are the best you could have in your cooking arsenal. They are not at all fragile, although they are quite light.
- Romertopf clay cookers
- Heavy-gauge aluminum half-sheet pans
- Aromatic wooden planks

### TEMPERING CLAY VESSELS

You'll need to temper vessels as they enter and exit your wood-burning oven to avoid a drastic temperature change that could damage them.

Maurice Yotnegparian of EarthStone Ovens suggests placing the filled dish near the oven door opening for 10 seconds. Turn the dish, letting it warm for another 10 seconds, then push it fully into the oven. Perform this tempering action in reverse when removing the hot dish from the oven.

### SEASONING AND CLEANING COOKWARE

Here are some general tips for seasoning clay, cast iron, and steel cookware. The seasoning forms a protective barrier against oxidation (rust) and it helps to keep food from sticking to the surface. Before using any cookware for the first time, make sure to follow the manufacturer's or artisan's directions for curing and care. Do not put any of the following kinds of cookware in a dishwasher or use an abrasive scrubber or cleanser to clean them.

**Seasoning cast iron:** Wash in slightly soapy water, dry, and rub with oil; place in a cold oven; heat to 350°F and bake for 2 hours. Turn off the heat and leave in the oven to cool down.

**Cleaning cast iron:** Never leave a cast-iron vessel in a sink filled with water. Gently wash with warm, slightly soapy water using a nylon scrubber; do not use steel wool or another kind of abrasive. Heavy scrubbing will remove the seasoning. Dry over direct heat to prevent rusting.

**Seasoning unglazed clay:** Before you use your clay cookware for the first time, be sure to follow the maker's instructions on seasoning. If there are no directions, use this method: Fill the piece with water and place it in a cold oven. Heat the oven to 400°F and bake uncovered for 30 minutes. Pour out the water and rub lightly with olive oil. This usually seals the cookware, although a complete seal is sometimes achieved only after it has been used for cooking several times. Boiling milk or vegetable oil in the vessel may help if it is found to be too porous still.

**Cleaning unglazed clay:** A quick soak and wipe down with a sponge is all that is generally needed. If more is needed, use a paste of baking soda and hot water as a gentle cleanser.

**Seasoning partially glazed clay:** Before using, soak the piece in water for 12 hours, then drain it and wipe it dry. Place in a preheated 250°F oven for about 20 minutes to thoroughly dry out. Some advise rubbing the glazed surface with a clove of garlic before drying in the oven to seal any unseen cracks in the glaze.

**Cleaning partially glazed clay:** Do not leave in standing water. A quick soak and wipe down with a sponge is all that is generally needed. If more is needed, use a paste of baking soda and hot water as a gentle cleanser.

**Seasoning carbon steel:** Carbon steel, like cast iron, is reactive to acidic foods and can rust (unlike stainless steel), so it needs to be seasoned before and after use. Carbon steel is also used for woks and paella pans, where high heat is required. Scrub your new pan in hot, soapy water to remove packing oils, then rinse well and towel dry. Set it over low direct heat for thorough drying, then let cool before seasoning.

Pour a bit of peanut, canola, or grapeseed oil into the pan and spread with your fingers over the inside surface up to the rim. Place the pan over medium heat until the oil begins to smoke. Let the pan cool completely. With a clean cloth or paper towel, wipe out any excess oil and your pan is now ready to use.

**Cleaning carbon steel:** After each use, clean your pan with very hot water and a scrubbing brush, then dry over low direct heat. If necessary, you can scour the pan first with table salt and a paper towel, or with baking soda. Do not use soap, as this will remove the seasoning, and the pan will have to be reseasoned. If your pan develops rust, simply sand out the rust, wash the pan thoroughly, and season it again.

### COOKING ON WOOD PLANKS

Planking, or plank cooking, is an ancient method that originated with Native Americans. The plank acts as a buffer to the fire allowing foods to roast or grill in their own juices and stay moist. The hardwood imparts its own distinct flavor as well as fragrant smoke to the food cooked on it. Food may be served directly on the charred plank. Although the flavors imparted by a given type of wood used as fuel or in plank form are similar, the complementary aspects of the wood changes slightly with different applications, so you'll see some small differences between these profiles and the hardwoods chart.

**Grilling planks** typically come in $\frac{3}{8}$- to $\frac{5}{8}$-inch thicknesses. They can be used up to 4 times. **Roasting planks** are $\frac{3}{4}$ to 1 inch thick to allow for a longer cooking time for roasting and resistance to the warping that can happen at high heat. These planks may be used 12 times, or until cracks form.

Alder, cedar, and hickory are the most popular woods for planking, though others are also used. Here is a list of common planking woods, their flavor profiles, and the foods they complement.

**Alder:** Mild wood flavor, with a soft smoky touch. Works well with most foods, especially seafood and vegetables.

**Cedar:** A robust and aromatic flavor. Complements salmon and spicy foods.

**Cherry:** Rich in flavor, with a touch of sweetness. Best suited to desserts.

**Hickory:** Strong smoky flavor. Good with beef, pork, and chicken with rubs or spicy marinades.

**Maple:** Mild sweet and smoky flavors. Good with beef, duck, and lamb, as well as fruit.

**Oak:** The same oaky flavor found in Chardonnay wine. Good with fish, game, beef, and lamb.

## Using Wood-Fired Appliances and Devices

The modern choices for cooking with wood run the gamut from the simplest campfire to the most elaborate permanent backyard oven. Here is a primer on the various ways of wood-fired cooking.

### Open-Fire Appliances and Devices

Other than some free-form styles of campfires, all open-fire appliances have some form of a vessel or cavity for housing the lump charcoal or firewood that protects the fire from drafts and contains the fire and ash. Each style of appliance has a different degree of efficiency, but all present more of an opportunity for spur-of-the-moment cooking than do wood-fired ovens. Cooking over an open fire allows you to make great-tasting food in less time than most other forms of wood-fired cookery.

Open-fire appliances include the basic campfire; the cowboy grill with a tripod suspension system for hanging pots over the fire; the open vessel fire pit; the fireplace; the open grate grill, such as the Aztec Grill; the tabletop grill, such as a hibachi; and the open grill of a box roaster.

#### CAMPFIRES AND VESSEL FIRE PITS

Traditional campfires are made from a circle of rocks or a square of bricks with a grill grate or spit suspended over them. Today there are free-standing, portable metal drum–like fire pits with grates and spark guard lids. Each can use either direct or indirect heat, and the cooking time can be either quick or extended with more fuel added or utilized until the fire dies out. To cook for an extended period of time over indirect heat, move the hot coals to one side or bank around the edges, and place the food on the center grate away from direct heat. Foods can be cooked over the fire, over the coals, or in the coals.

#### Equipment and Accessories for Campfires or Vessel Fire Pits

**For general use:** multilevel grates, for cooking multiple foods at the same time; Tuscan grill insertion, for grilling; pizza screens or perforated pans, for roasting peppers or delicate vegetables such as tomatillos; stainless kebab set and frame, for cooking skewered meats or fruits; tripod suspension system, for hanging pots over the fire; battery-operated or hand-cranked spit rotisserie; roasting drum basket accessory for the spit rotisserie; grilling planks.

**For grilling:** Grill grate, pizza stone, wood planks.

**For spit-roasting:** A battery-operated or hand-cranked spit rotisserie for roasting large cuts of meats, whole chickens, or even a pineapple (see recipe page 174) and an added roasting drum basket attachment, for roasting peppers, popcorn, or coffee.

#### FIREPLACE

A fireplace is a three-sided chamber with a flue. They may be found both inside and outside the house. They can use both direct and indirect heat, for either grilling or roasting. Foods that can be cooked in a fireplace include pizza and flatbreads, steaks and ribs, poultry and game, and kebabs.

## Equipment and Accessories for Fireplaces

**For general use:** multilevel grates, for cooking multiple foods at the same time; pizza screens or perforated pans, for roasting peppers or delicate vegetables such as tomatillos; stainless kebab set and frame, for cooking skewered meats or fruits; grilling planks; Tuscan grill insertion, for grilling; fireplace hearth grate, which sits inside the fireplace to hold the firewood.

**For grilling:** Grill grate or Tuscan grill, pizza stone or heat diffuser, aromatic wood planks.

**For spit-roasting:** A battery-operated, hand-cranked, or electric spit rotisserie or with an added roasting drum basket attachment.

### KETTLE, DRUM/BARREL, AND BOX GRILLS

Kettle grills are the most popular style of grill in this country, but drum grills (also called barrel grills) and box grills are also familiar to most Americans and function on the same heating principles: A fire is built in the well of the kettle, drum, or box, then a grill grate is placed above the fire; a lid can be used to improve heat circulation and reduce flare-ups. Drum grills are typically larger than kettle grills; in their simplest form, they are just a large steel barrel cut in half lengthwise. Box grills refer to large steel fireboxes that tend to be better insulated than kettle or drum grills. Each style can use direct and indirect heat, for either grilling or roasting. Foods can be cooked over the fire, over the coals, or in the coals.

## Equipment and Accessories for Kettle, Drum, and Box Grills

**For general use:** multilevel grates, for cooking multiple foods at the same time; pizza screens or perforated pans, for roasting peppers or delicate vegetables such as tomatillos; stainless kebab set and frame, for cooking skewered meats or fruits; battery-operated or hand-cranked spit rotisserie; roasting drum basket accessory for the spit rotisserie; grilling planks.

**For grilling:** Pizza stone, wood planks.

**For spit-roasting:** A battery-operated or hand-cranked spit rotisserie for roasting large cuts of meats, whole chickens, or even a pineapple (see recipe page 174) and an added roasting drum basket attachment for roasting peppers, popcorn, or coffee.

## Building an Open Fire

Each style and brand of open-fire appliance will have its own recommendations for fire building, but here is general information to get you started using the most popular equipment.

Start the fire using a nontoxic starter and a few strips of kindling. Place 2 to 3 pieces of starter in between the kindling and light them. After the fire catches, add a few small split logs or lump charcoal on top. Add additional fuel as needed for the desired heat fire. If using lump charcoal, a charcoal chimney is a useful tool to get the coals hot and glowing. To use a charcoal chimney, stuff the bottom of the chimney with one sheet of newspaper. Through the top, fill the chimney with chunks of lump charcoal and set on the bottom grate of the grill. Light the newspaper and leave the chimney uncovered until the coals are glowing red and some are light grey. Empty the lighted charcoal into the fuel bed or lower grate and place small split logs or more lump charcoal on top. Add more fuel as needed. Some cookers that can be used as a grill, such as the Big Green Egg, and hardwood-burning grills, such as the Aztec Grill, do not require started charcoal. When using these appliances, simply place lump charcoal or hardwood in the base of the cooker and light.

Once the flames have burned down, you can gauge the heat of the fire both by appearance and by feel. The coals will be glowing red with some light grey areas. Some charcoal grills have thermometers attached to help determine when the desired temperature is achieved. Without a thermometer, you'll need to use the "hand test": Hold your open hand 6 to 8 inches above the heat source and count the number of seconds that it takes until the heat forces you to pull your hand away. If you pulled away after 1 to 2 seconds, the fire is red hot and used for searing; a 3-second fire is medium-hot, for cooking small pieces of food quickly; a 4- or 5-second fire is medium, for cooking moderate size pieces; and a 6-second fire indicates medium-low to low temperatures, which are appropriate for cooking larger, denser pieces of food.

To cook using indirect heat, move hot coals off to one side or bank around the perimeter of the appliance. With some cookers, such as the Big Green Egg, indirect cooking is created by inserting a plate setter or a ceramic pizza stone in the oven to create a barrier from the fuel. To cook using direct heat, leave the hot embers directly under the grill grate. Add fresh fuel as needed to maintain the desired temperature range. Add the new fuel to the heated embers on one side of the appliance, then disperse the embers over the cooking area. If using a charcoal chimney, keep a second one loaded and ready as a backup in case you see the fire dying down and needing more fuel.

## Wood-Fired Ovens

Today's wood-fired ovens are based on ancient oven styles and cooking practices, improved on by modern technology. These highly efficient ovens offer three ways of cooking food: direct heat (heat from the fuel source), convection heat (hot air circulated around the food), and radiant, or induction, heat (heat radiated from the oven mass). Direct heat means the fire is left in the oven cavity while food is cooked (as in a pizza oven or tandoor oven), and radiant heat means that the fire is removed before food is placed in the oven and the absorbed heat radiating from the structure cooks the food. Convection heat is a rolling heat that is the result of the fire's location and the shape of the oven dome. It's desirable for creating top color on certain foods, such as pizza. The method chosen is based on the food that is being cooked and the desired results.

Wood-fired ovens can be made of fire bricks and masonry, precast high-density refractory clay, soapstone, stone hearth cast ceramic, or space-age ceramics. They either are the horizontal "Roman" dome shape or are vertical in shape, like a tandoor. Dome ovens have a door and front flue or flue out the door opening; examples include the Italian *forno*, or pizza oven, the beehive oven, the Native American *horno*, and the European bread oven. Vertical ovens are bottom-fueled, made of clay shaped into a cylinder, with an open top. Dome ovens are used to bake hearth breads, pizzas, and flatbreads, and for roasting and baking. They can also be used for grilling by inserting a cast-iron grate or Tuscan grill into the chamber. Vertical ovens may be used for flatbread baking and grilling.

With proper planning and enough retained heat, in one firing of an oven you can make simple, flavorful food for a family of four for an entire week; doing so much more efficiently than you can in a conventional oven by having the ability to cook while the oven cools down over a long period (see Chapter 3).

The major difference between a wood-fired oven and a conventional oven is that the wood-fired oven does not have an on-demand heat source. It requires a bit of planning about what you want to cook and when you want to eat it. Depending on its size and construction, the desired temperature, and the chosen fuel, a wood-fired oven can take anywhere from one to six hours to heat properly. If an oven is used every few days, there will be some retained heat in its mass and it will therefore take less time and fuel to heat at the next firing. This is one reason why it makes good sense to use your wood-fired oven on a regular basis.

Wood-fired ovens vary in the level of their heat retention (also known as heat sink), which depends on the kind of material the oven is made of and the amount of insulation the oven has. Some ovens are designed to heat up quickly, which can mean, of course, that they can also cool down more quickly. The more heat-retentive an oven is, the less fuel is required to maintain its heat. The more heat the oven cavity can hold and radiate, the longer and more efficiently the oven will maintain the desired temperature. With sufficient heat retention or heat sink, you have more available cooking time and therefore more cooking options. This reserved heat allows for making many consecutive dishes from one firing. As the oven cools, you can cook dishes that require less heat. Try something simple, like Overnight Beef Chile Colorado (page 157), which is cooked in a cooling wood-fired oven. You'll not only have the best chile you've ever tasted the next day, but you'll better understand how easy it is to cook this way.

### Equipment and Accessories for Wood-Fired Ovens

**For general use:** Hearth grate, cast-iron grill pans, ceramic pizza stones, multilevel grates, grilling and roasting planks.

**For oven-roasting:** Two to four fire bricks, restaurant-quality baking sheets, wire racks, terracotta bakeware, small paella pans.

**For drying:** Four to six fire bricks, aluminum pizza screens, perforated pizza pans, wire racks, sheets of stainless steel mesh.

### Firing and Monitoring Wood-Fired Ovens

Each style and brand of wood-fired oven will have its own recommendations for fire building, but here is general information to get you started regardless of the brand of equipment.

When using a wood-fired oven, build your fire in the center, set back about 8 inches from the door. Use a couple of pieces of wadded-up brown paper bags and six or so small pieces of kindling along with a few nontoxic starters. Leave the door open, as the fire needs oxygen to burn successfully.

Once the fire has caught, add a couple of small pieces of hardwood (about 3 inches in diameter) and continue to do so every 20 minutes or so. When the fire gets going, the flames should reach the center to the front of the oven dome, but not reach too far out into the oven opening (which would send precious heat out the flue).

After about 40 minutes, the roof of the oven will start to turn clear or white (see the photo on page 29); this visual cue, called a "bloom," means that the carbon deposited on the dome has begun to be burned off and that the oven is hot enough to have the fire expanded. When this occurs, start building your fire outward by adding small logs to the sides of the burning fuel and toward the back, creating a larger footprint over the floor of the oven. This wider fire will drive the heat across the entire cooking floor and the dome. At this point, the floor of the oven, which is the cooking area, has reached at least 700°F, the desired high temperature for foods requiring quick cooking, such as pizza. The embers or ash should be spread over the floor for about 10 minutes to even out the temperature of the floor. Then clear the floor, shoving the embers to the rear of the oven, and proceed to bake goods directly on the oven floor. Some ovens require that a small fire be kept burning in the rear of the oven to maintain the desired temperature or the convection of lapping flames over the food. In this case, use some of the hot embers as a base for starting a small fire with one or two small logs. Brush the remaining ash from the floor and into a heat-resistant ash bucket to cool. In either case, there is no need to swab the floor with a wet rag to clean it; a little residual ash won't harm you. If not baking directly on the cleared oven floor, leave some embers in the center and place a cast-iron grate or Tuscan grill over them to create a raised area for grilling or to use as a rack for placing casseroles on.

Wood-fired ovens typically do not need a lot of attention once the fire is going. While you are waiting for the oven to heat, you can be using that time to do other tasks around the house or prepare the food to be cooked. Just check in with the fire every 20 minutes or so to add more fuel as needed to obtain the desired temperature. Check the oven temperature on a regular basis using the oven's imbedded probes, a hand-held laser thermometer, or the old-fashioned baker's technique of throwing a small amount of flour onto the floor of the oven to see how long it takes for the flour to turn tan, brown, or black. If the flour burns right away, it's probably at 700°F or more and ready for baking pizza. If it turns dark brown in a few seconds, the oven is probably at 500°F or more and in the range for baking bread.

If it turns tan in a few seconds, it's probably in the 400°F range and ready for roasting.

## Ceramic Cookers, Smokers, and Box Roasters

These appliances are separated out because of their popularity and uniqueness in shape and cooking abilities. A ceramic cooker is a multifunction smoker-oven-grill, a cross between an insulated wood-fired grill and a wood-burning oven. These cookers have the best characteristics of both: superior insulation with retained and radiant heat. The Big Green Egg ceramic cooker is a particularly efficient combination cooker-smoker-grill that utilizes lump charcoal; it has a range of controllable temperatures from low-smoking to high-pizza baking. Due to its efficiency, it uses far less fuel than other grills. Using both the direct and indirect heat methods of cooking in a ceramic cooker is ideal for slow-roasting meats, poultry, fish, and vegetables because the low temperatures are easily maintained. At higher temperatures, ceramic cooker like the Big Green Egg can be used as an oven or a grill.

Smokers and box roasters are basically ovens and function as such. Smokers are vented, while box roasters are not because the food is enclosed in a cooking cavity with the fuel source on top. Both types of appliance cook food by indirect and convection heat or smoke at low temperatures and usually require little attention from the cook once food is placed in the cooker. Some drum-style or vertical grills can be used as smokers or have side smoker chambers attached. Smokers and box roasters use either wood chips, wood pellets, fruitwood, or lump charcoal as fuel for cooking and flavoring. They allow for long, slow cooking, which is best for roasted meats, fish, and vegetables.

TODAY'S FIRE PIT: LA CAJA CHINA BOX ROASTER

Although in-ground fire pits are still used around the world, today's box roasters are an ideal way to emulate pit cooking and have the advantage of being a self-contained device. The box roaster known as La Caja China is a simple metal-lined roaster-smoker with its heat source of charcoal or hardwood located above the food being cooked. It cooks with indirect heat at relatively low temperatures, capturing the moisture from the food roasting in the metal-lined box. Though traditionally used for roasting meats—from a whole pig to multiple chickens—fish and vegetables roasted this way are also sensational.

## Firing Ceramic Cookers, Smokers, and Box Roasters

As stated previously, most cookers, smokers, and box roasters do not require started charcoal. When using these appliances, simply place lump charcoal in the base of the cooker (or on top, in the case of box roasters) and light according to manufacturer's instructions.

To maintain the desired temperature, either use vents on the appliance to control the temperature (with ceramic cookers such as the Big Green Egg) or adjust fuel by adding more or moving coals aside (with smokers and box roasters). Depending on your brand and style of cooker, you might need to attach or insert a smoker chamber.

## Equipment and Accessories for Ceramic Cookers, Smokers, and Box Roasters

**For general use:** Hearth grate, cast-iron grill pans, ceramic pizza stones, multilevel grates, grilling and roasting planks.

**For smoking:** Carbon steel wok, lid, and burner ring; two to four fire bricks; aluminum pizza screens; perforated pizza pans; sheets of stainless steel mesh; baking sheet; cast-iron smoker box; heavy-duty aluminum foil.

**For roasting or grilling:** Grill grate, rotisserie.

As the wood-fired cooking trend continues to grow, even more good-quality wood-burning devices rooted in historical cooking methods will continue to be developed. The appliances covered here are my favorites, but I encourage you to experiment with a variety of wood-fired cookers, grills, and ovens to see which one best fits your needs.

Aztec grill

Big Green Egg shown with tandoor skewers

Drum roasting basket

Built-in masonry oven

Building fire in vessel fire pit

Florentine Grill

## CHAPTER 3

# Becoming an Efficient Wood-Fire Cook

Wouldn't you love to cook just once a week and be able to feed your family multiple meals? Just imagine a scenario where you fire your wood-burning oven on a Sunday morning and in the late afternoon family and friends gather, each bringing one dish to be cooked in the oven, each dish large enough to feed all the people present at that day's meal and into the week. You fire *one* oven, cook all the food over the course of a few hours, and while the food is cooking you are spending quality social time with loved ones. When the food is ready, you share some of the food at the community table and then divide the balance among the families so each can take home delicious food to eat for the week. In that process you have created not just nourishment for all who are present, but a sense of community among the group.

## Develop a Cooking Plan

Executing a successful meal takes some forethought and planning. Following are the basic steps to take for planning and managing your wood-fired cooking. Refer to the chart on page 8 for examples of appliances and heating timelines.

1. Determine the available time for food preparation and cooking.

   *Do you have one hour until mealtime or do you have most of the day?*

2. Choose the appliance needed for creating food within the available time.

   *Do you need to use a grill that takes little time to heat, or do you have time to fire the wood-burning oven?*

3. Determine whether the cooking session will be for one meal or multiple meals.

   *Do you need to keep it to one dish or meal because mealtime is soon or can you make one or more meals over the course of the day?*

4. Create a basic menu and prepare an easy-to-follow cooking schedule based on the chosen appliance and available time. The sample menu below will help to guide you in your planning.

### Sample Menu

Depending upon the appliances used, the time available for cooking, and the number of people you are feeding, here's a sample menu for your wood-fired cooking session.

| One Week's Worth of Food | | |
|---|---|---|
| DISH | APPLIANCE | COOKING TIME & TEMPERATURE |
| Hearth breads | Wood-fired oven | 25 minutes at 650°F |
| Mushroom-Artichoke Ragout | Wood-fired oven or cooker | 15 to 20 minutes at 350° to 375°F |
| Grilled Pork Loin Stuffed with Chard, Fennel, and Olives | Wood-fired grill | 20 minutes at 450°F |
| Smoky French Onion Soup | Wood-fired oven or cooker | 10 to 15 minutes at 400°F |
| White Tuscan Beans with Sausage | Wood-fired oven or indirect heat on grill | 1 hour at 350°F or overnight at 250°F or lower as the oven cools down |
| Smoky Tomato Sauce | Wood-fired oven or grill | 35 minutes at 400°F or overnight at 250°F or lower as the oven cools down |
| Succulent Smoked Salmon | Wood-fired oven on grate, in grill, or in vertical ceramic cooker | 30 to 35 minutes at 190°F |

| Complete Meal One | | |
|---|---|---|
| DISH | APPLIANCE | COOKING TIME & TEMPERATURE |
| Pizza | Wood-fired oven | 7 to 10 minutes at 600° to 700°F |
| Chicken Toscana Cooked Under Bricks | Wood-fired oven on floor | 30 minutes at 450°F |
| Eggplant, Red Pepper, and Goat Cheese Gratin | Wood-fired oven | 25 minutes at 400°F |
| Apple-Prune Galette | Wood-fired oven on floor | 25 to 30 minutes at 450°F |

| Complete Meal Two | | |
|---|---|---|
| DISH | APPLIANCE | COOKING TIME & TEMPERATURE |
| Grilled Shrimp | Wood-fired grill | 5 minutes at 450°F |
| Grilled Cilantro-Mint Naan | Wood-fired grill | 5 minutes at 450°F |
| Tandoori Chicken | Wood-fired grill | 25 minutes at 500°F |
| Grilled Dessert Pizza | Wood-fired grill | 10 minutes at 425°F |

## Intentional Leftovers

When developing a cooking plan to make efficient use of a single firing, remember that one simple dish could equal multiple subsequent dishes: one spit-roasted lemon-herb chicken could be used to make Smoked Chicken and Herb Dumplings, Pita sandwiches, chicken and escarole soup, and lemon-herb chicken and feta pasta salad.

Keep in mind that these tables are only suggestions. Other appliances can be used in the place of those listed. If an oven is suggested, a covered wood-fired grill or vertical ceramic cooker, such as the Big Green Egg, can also be used.

## Adapting Recipes to Wood-Fired Cooking Environments

Wood-fired ovens and cookers cook food at about the same rate as in conventional cooking environments at comparable temperatures, so, although all of the recipes in this book were created specifically for wood-fired cooking, you can also make "normal" recipes on your wood-fired appliance. But, because of the intensity of the heat, you will need to rotate the pans or cookware more frequently than in a conventional gas or electric oven.

For example, a "normal" recipe that calls for roasting in a conventional oven at 350°F translates to cooking over *indirect* heat, 8 to 10 inches from the heat source, on a grill or *indirect convection* heat, 8 to 10 inches from the heat source, in a 350°F wood-burning oven or cooker.

Below is a chart that will help you to adapt conventional recipes for wood-fired cooking.

Now that you have some basic guidelines and the proper tools at hand, it's time to dive in and gather friends to share great food. The cooking chapters in this book are organized by the heat of the fire and

cooking methods, so you'll learn how to cook at the highest available heat as well at the lowest possible temperatures. All of the recipes have been prepared on a variety of wood-fired appliances; you should feel free to make them on whichever appliance you own. As you experiment with these recipes and recommendations, you will surely discover even more exciting ways to cook with fire and incorporate those into your cooking repertoire. As I often tell students in my cooking classes, these recipes are only guidelines; think of them as road maps to other dishes and flavor discoveries.

## Adapting Recipes for Wood-Fired Cooking

| TECHNIQUE | CONDITIONS | TEMPERATURE RANGE |
| --- | --- | --- |
| Baking | Enclosed environment; indirect heat | High temperatures (650° to 900°F) for bread or flatbreads; 450°F for tarts or dishes with more delicate crusts |
| Grilling | Enclosed or open environment; direct and indirect heat | 450° to 500°F |
| Roasting | Enclosed environment; indirect heat | 325° to 350°F |
| Braising | Simmering in a small amount of liquid, usually in an enclosed environment; indirect heat | 300° to 325°F |
| Pit or box roasting | Enclosed environment; indirect heat | 200° to 275°F |
| Poaching | Gently cooking in a liquid kept just under boiling point | 190° to 210°F |
| Hot Smoking | Cooking and smoking simultaneously; indirect heat | 130° to 225°F |
| Drying | Enclosed environment; indirect heat | 125° to 140°F |

# CHAPTER 4

# Baking Flatbreads
# and Rustic Artisan Breads

Every culture has some form of bread. In its most primitive form, it is simple and basic: made by hand using flour, water, and salt. It's no wonder that bread is referred to as the staff of life, as bread made from whole grains combined with other nutritional ingredients can indeed sustain life. Even thin flatbreads are hearty and nourishing. It's hard to resist any freshly baked breads, especially those baked in a wood-fired oven.

Bread is the oldest food baked in wood-fired ovens. The artisan breads and flatbreads we are most familiar with today in the United States are derived from the traditional breads of Europe. I've included a few basic dough recipes for making the most popular flatbreads, such as pizza, focaccia, and calzone, as well as recipes for some of my favorite rustic artisan breads. These breads are especially wonderful when baked by the heat of a wood fire.

The high temperatures of a wood-fired oven provide the perfect environment for loaves to spring and form a crispy crust, a good crumb structure and optimum caramelization and flavor development. For flatbreads, because they are thin, there is an almost instant caramelization and formation of crispy crusts.

## Baking Guidelines

In a wood-fired oven, loaf breads bake with the coals removed from the oven. Depending on the heat retention of your oven, the coals should be removed 45 minutes to 2 hours before baking, allowing the heat in the cavity to be absorbed thoroughly into the walls, floor, and ceiling.

For flatbreads, spread the embers out over the floor of the oven and leave for 20 minutes for the heat to be evenly distributed. Push the embers to the side rear of the oven and keep a small fire of one log going while baking.

In a ceramic kamado-style cooker such as the Big Green Egg, the hot coals remain in the bottom. The desired temperature is 500°F for loaf breads and 600° to 650°F for flatbreads. A ceramic buffer insert is used to create an indirect baking environment, essentially turning the appliance into an oven. The bread or flatbread is baked on a hot pizza stone, which has absorbed the heat of the cooker.

To cook these recipes in a conventional oven: Preheat the oven to the highest available temperature. Bake rustic loaf breads in a clay cloche or on a pizza stone. Flatbreads should be baked on a pizza stone or clay tiles. Fire brick pavers are the best option because they are better heat conductors, and because not all clay tiles will hold up at high temperatures. To make your oven more heat efficient, keep a layer of fire brick pavers on the top and bottom racks of the oven. For loaf breads, add steam to the baking environment by filling a baking sheet or a small cast-iron pot with hot water.

# Basic Pizza Dough

Every baker has a favorite pizza recipe, and this one is mine. This is one of the easiest pizza doughs you can make, and it can be used for calzones, too.

MAKES ENOUGH DOUGH FOR 4 INDIVIDUAL PIZZAS

2 teaspoons active dry yeast
4 cups unbleached all-purpose flour
2 teaspoons kosher salt
1½ cups water, or more as needed
Olive oil, for brushing

Using a stand mixer fitted with a dough hook attachment, mix the yeast, flour, and salt on low speed for 2 minutes, then gradually add the 1½ cups water. Increase the speed to medium and mix for 5 minutes, then return to low speed for another 2 minutes to start the creation of gluten. Add up to ½ cup more water as needed to make a dough that pulls away from the walls of the mixer bowl and is slightly tacky to the touch. (The ambient humidity will affect how much water is needed.)

On a lightly floured board, form the dough into a ball. Place in an oiled bowl and turn the dough to coat it with oil. Cover the bowl with a damp cloth or plastic wrap and let the dough rise in a warm place until doubled in bulk, about 2 hours. For additional flavor, put the dough in a sealed container and let bulk overnight in the refrigerator. Allow dough to come to room temperature (about 1 hour) before punching down and forming into a ball. Punch it down, then empty the dough out onto a lightly floured board, form into a ball, and cut it into 4 equal pieces. Shape each piece into a ball by gently stretching then rolling the ball and tucking the dough under on the bottom. (Bakers refer to this as the bread's "belly button.") Set each ball on a well-floured baking sheet and lightly brush the top of each ball with olive oil. Cover loosely with a towel or plastic wrap. Let rise for at least 1 hour, until doubled in size. Refrigerate if not using immediately. Or, place each ball of dough in an oiled self-sealing plastic bag and refrigerate for up to 3 days, or freeze for up to 1 month. Allow refrigerated dough to stand at room temperature for 1 hour before using. Thaw frozen dough in the bag at room temperature until dough warms up and has risen to almost twice its size.

# Pizza al Forno with Mushrooms, Gorgonzola, and Radicchio

This pizza could be named Umami Pizza because it features the earthy flavors of mushrooms and Gorgonzola cheese. The radicchio provides a slightly bitter flavor for contrast and adds color. Sautéing the mushrooms and garlic in the wood-fired oven adds an additional layer of flavor.

MAKES 4 INDIVIDUAL PIZZAS

3 tablespoons olive oil, plus more for brushing and drizzling

1 pound cremini or white mushrooms, thinly sliced

3 cloves garlic, thinly sliced

1 head red radicchio, cored and cut into 1-inch wedges

2 tablespoons balsamic vinegar or Saba

Basic Pizza Dough (page 33)

Coarse sea salt, for sprinkling

2 tablespoons fresh thyme leaves

12 ounces Gorgonzola or other blue cheese, crumbled

Prepare a very hot fire (650° to 700°F) in a wood-fired oven or cooker.

In a cast-iron skillet or heat-resistant baking dish, heat the 3 tablespoons olive oil over medium heat and sauté the mushrooms for 5 minutes, then add the garlic and sauté for another 5 minutes. Remove from the heat and let cool.

In a medium-sized bowl, toss the radicchio with the balsamic vinegar.

Flour a baking peel and shape each dough ball into a 10-inch round on the peel. Brush with olive oil, being careful not to get oil on the peel. Sprinkle lightly with sea salt. Leaving a ½-inch border of crust, top with the mushrooms, then the radicchio, thyme, and Gorgonzola. Drizzle with olive oil (including the edges) and sprinkle again with sea salt.

Slide the pizzas off the peel and onto the oven floor. Bake for 7 to 10 minutes, rotating once, or until golden on the edges and the cheese is melted. Let cool for 5 minutes, then cut into wedges and serve.

# Focaccia with Oven-Roasted Tomatoes, Ricotta Salata, and Basil Oil

Focaccia is one of the easiest flatbreads to make: No shaping is needed because the dough is stretched and spread out in the sheet pan. This recipe uses a very wet dough, resulting in a moist flatbread about 3/4 inch thick. You can substitute shavings of Parmesan for the ricotta salata cheese, if you like. Focaccia is best eaten the day it is baked.

**MAKES ONE 12 BY 17-INCH FOCACCIA**

### DOUGH

2 1/2 teaspoons active dry yeast

2 cups warm water

3/4 cup olive oil, plus more for drizzling

1 tablespoon fennel seeds soaked in 2 tablespoons
    warm water

4 cups unbleached all-purpose flour

2 teaspoons kosher salt

Coarse sea salt, for sprinkling

### TOPPINGS

Basil Oil, for drizzling (recipe follows)

Oven-Roasted Tomatoes (page 187)

1 1/2 cups coarsely chopped mixed fresh herbs: basil, mint,
    chives, oregano, and/or summer savory

6 ounces ricotta salata cheese, crumbled or cut into
    shavings

To make the dough, sprinkle the yeast over the warm water in a bowl and stir to dissolve the yeast. Let stand until foamy, about 10 minutes. Add 1/2 cup of the olive oil and the fennel seeds along with their liquid.

Mix the flour and salt in a large bowl or in the bowl of a stand mixer. Gradually add the yeast mixture to the dry ingredients and mix until well incorporated. If using a stand mixer, use a dough hook on low speed. Mix until the dough comes away from the sides of the bowl. No kneading is necessary for this flatbread.

Place the dough in a lightly oiled large bowl, turning the dough to coat with oil. Cover the bowl with a damp towel or plastic wrap and place in a warm spot to rise until doubled in size, 1 to 1 1/2 hours. Using a dough scraper, fold the dough two times and cover to rise until doubled in size again, about 1 hour. Or, for more flavor, cover and refrigerate the dough overnight. Remove from the refrigerator 1 to 2 hours before shaping and let come to room temperature.

Prepare a hot fire (450° to 475°F) in a wood-fired oven or grill. If using an oven, keep a small fire (one small log) going in the left rear of the oven. This will help to maintain the desired temperature and add flavor to the focaccia.

Lightly brush a 12 by 17-inch rimmed baking sheet with olive oil. Line with a sheet of parchment paper and brush generously with olive oil, making sure you oil the sides of the pan. Place the dough on the prepared pan and stretch to cover as much of the pan as possible. Using your fingertips, dimple the top and stretch the dough more. This very wet dough will not hold all of the dimple marks, but that's okay. Some dimples will remain, and they will hold the drizzled oil. Cover with a dry towel and set aside to relax for 15 minutes.

Drizzle the dough with 1/4 cup of the olive oil. Dimple the dough again and sprinkle with coarse sea salt. Place in the middle of the wood-fired oven, about 8 inches from the small fire. Bake, rotating once or twice, until golden brown, 20 to 25 minutes. Remove from the oven and drizzle with the Basil Oil.

continued

Place on a wire rack to cool for 10 minutes. Top with the tomatoes, herbs, and cheese. Cut into serving-size squares or rectangles and serve.

## BASIL OIL

### MAKES APPROXIMATELY 2½ CUPS

2 cups tightly packed fresh basil leaves (about 1 bunch)
1 cup extra-virgin olive oil

In a large saucepan of salted boiling water, blanch the basil for 5 seconds. Drain and plunge the herbs into a bowl of ice water. Drain well and squeeze out all the liquid.

Puree in a blender with the olive oil. Cover and let stand overnight. Strain through a fine double-mesh sieve. Pour into a sterilized glass bottle or plastic squeeze bottle, seal, and refrigerate for up to 1 month, though it is best used within 1 week.

## Community Cooking in Priscilla Hoback's *Horno*

Priscilla Hoback is a well-known native Santa Fean potter and sculptor who I was introduced to by her neighbor, Deborah Madison. Priscilla's family owned the legendary Pink Adobe restaurant in Santa Fe for many years. As a potter, she knows fire well. It's no wonder that she would build a Native American *horno* on her compound outside of Santa Fe. It's made from slabs of a form of silica (found on her property) at the base, then fire bricks for the floor; the dome is a mixture of clay (also from her property) and straw. After building the *horno*, Priscilla went on to make her own cooking pots from New Mexican micaceous clay. One late spring day, a group of friends and neighbors gathered in her kitchen to cook together in the *horno*. The flavors and aromas of the food we cooked that day in Priscilla's handmade clay pots were amazing! Nothing beats a wood-fire-cooked feast eaten with friends around a big community table.

# Calzone with Sausage, Spinach, Fontina, and Pine Nuts

This is one of my favorite savory calzones because the filling is so delicious. The sausage and onions become smoky because they are first cooked in the wood-fired oven. Spinach is a natural with these two ingredients. The creamy, slightly nutty fontina cheese is a great companion to the toasted pine nuts. This combination would be wonderful on a pizza as well.

MAKES 8 CALZONES

2 tablespoons olive oil, plus more for brushing

2 red onions, cut into thin wedges

12 ounces sweet Italian sausage, removed from casings
    and crumbled

8 large cloves garlic, peeled

2 cups packed spinach leaves

1/4 teaspoon red pepper flakes

Basic Pizza Dough (page 33)

2 tablespoons coarsely chopped fresh mint

2 cups shredded Italian fontina cheese

1 cup pine nuts, toasted in olive oil (page 184)

Coarse sea salt

Prepare a very hot fire (650°F) in a wood-fired oven or cooker.

Put the 2 tablespoons olive oil in a high-heat-proof terra-cotta baking dish or cast-iron skillet. Add the onions, sausage, and garlic. Place in the center of the wood-fired oven to cook until the sausage is lightly crisped and the onions and garlic are well caramelized, about 15 minutes. Remove from the oven and stir in the spinach and red pepper flakes. Set aside to cool slightly.

When ready to form the dough, flour a baking peel and shape each dough ball into an 8-inch round on the peel. Lightly brush the dough with olive oil without getting the oil on the peel. Spread the filling on half of the dough, leaving ¾ inch on the edge. Add the mint, then sprinkle with the cheese and pine nuts. Lightly salt.

Fold the dough over the filling, matching up the edges. Fold the edges over to further seal and crimp closed with a fork. Lightly brush the top with olive oil and lightly sprinkle with sea salt. Let rest for 10 minutes.

Slide the calzones onto the floor of the wood-fired oven, 8 to 10 inches away from the heat source, and bake, turning occasionally for even color, until they are puffed and golden, 10 to 15 minutes. Let cool for 5 minutes, then cut in half and serve.

# Mt. Taylor Five-Seed Sourdough Bread

Tim Decker and his wife, Crystal, are the owners of Bennett Valley Bakery in Sonoma County. A former apprentice of Peter Reinhart's, Tim makes artisan breads with a beautifully browned crust by baking them in a wood-fired oven at unusually high temperatures. You can also make this bread successfully in a conventional oven, with the heat as high as it will go.

MAKES 4 TO 6 LOAVES

28 ounces (about 3½ cups) Sourdough Starter
    (recipe follows)
¼ cup buttermilk
¼ cup rye flour
¼ cup whole-wheat flour
5 cups high protein flour
¾ cup plus ½ cup seed mix (flax, sesame, pumpkin,
    sunflower, poppy)
1 tablespoon kosher salt
1½ cups warm water (82°F)

In a stand mixer, combine the starter and buttermilk at a low speed until incorporated. Combine the flours and ¾ cup of the seed mix in a large mixing bowl. With the mixer on slow speed, add ¼ of the dry ingredients into the starter mixture. Repeat with the remaining 3 batches, then mix for 6 minutes, until all of the flour is incorporated. Add the salt and mix for 2 more minutes.

Transfer the dough to a large, clear plastic container, cover, and proof at room temperature for approximately 2 hours, until the dough has doubled in size.

Prepare a very hot fire (575° to 600°F) in a wood-fired oven, preferably with oak. Keep a small fire going in one corner. The lowest temperature at which bread can be baked is 475°F.

Line 4 to 6 9-inch round or oval baskets with floured linen or a flour sack or dust with flour. Once the dough has doubled from its original size, liberally sprinkle the counter with flour (about ½ cup) then gently trans-

fer the dough to the floured counter. Dip a metal pastry scraper into cool water to keep it from sticking to the dough, then scale the dough into 1- to 1½-pound pieces. Dip your hands in flour to keep the dough from sticking, then shape each piece into a round and place in the prepared baskets.

Refrigerate tightly covered for later use, or proof again at room temperature for 1½ hours, until the rounds have doubled in size. Spread the remaining seed mix on a baking sheet and roll the top of each loaf in the seed mix.

Place the rounds directly on the floor of the oven and bake, rotating once or twice, for 15 to 20 minutes, until the loaves are toasty, browned all over, and have a hollow sound when thumped on the bottom. Remove from the heat and place on a wire rack. Let cool for 1 hour before slicing.

## SOURDOUGH STARTER

3½ tablespoons whole-wheat or rye flour
¼ cup unsweetened pineapple juice or filtered or spring
    water, at room temperature (about 70°F)

Five days before you bake bread, in a small bowl, stir together the flour and juice with a spoon or whisk to make a paste. It should be like pancake batter. Be sure to stir until all of the flour is hydrated. Cover loosely with

plastic wrap and leave at room temperature for about 48 hours. Two or three times a day, aerate by stirring for 1 minute with a wet spoon or whisk.

Three days before you bake, feed ¼ cup of your original starter with 1 cup water (at about 75°F), 1 cup unbleached flour, and ¼ cup whole-wheat flour (discard any unused original starter). After 4 hours, feed with 2 cups water (at about 75°F), 2 cups unbleached flour, and ½ cup whole-wheat flour. After 4 to 6 more hours, feed with 4 cups water (at about 75°F), 4 cups unbleached flour, and 1 cup whole-wheat flour. Tightly cover with

plastic wrap and let sit at room temperature for 8 to 16 hours to proof.

Two days before you bake, discard half of the starter and repeat feedings, as above.

One day before you bake, discard half of the starter and repeat feedings, as above.

On baking day, measure out starter needed and set aside some starter to be used the next time. Discard extra starter or give to baker friends. Cover and refrigerate reserved starter for up to 2 weeks or freeze for 6 months. Bring to room temperature before using.

# Moroccan Flatbread Stuffed with Onion, Parsley, and Cumin

This multilayered flatbread is made by spreading the dough with the filling, then folding, rolling, and cooking quickly on both sides on a hot cast-iron griddle or stone. I love to serve them as an appetizer and often add a bit of salty crumbled cheese such as sheep's milk feta to the filling.

MAKES 8 FLATBREADS

$^1/_2$ teaspoon active dry yeast

$^1/_4$ cup warm water (105° to 115°F)

2 cups unbleached all-purpose flour, plus more for kneading

1 teaspoon kosher salt, plus more for seasoning

1 yellow onion, very finely chopped

$^1/_2$ cup minced fresh flat-leaf parsley

3 tablespoons unsalted butter, at room temperature

1 teaspoon sweet Hungarian paprika

$^1/_2$ teaspoon ground cumin

5 ounces brined cheese, such as sheep's milk feta (optional)

Prepare a hot fire (475°F) in a wood-fired oven or grill.

Sprinkle the yeast over the warm water in a small bowl and stir to dissolve the yeast. Let stand until foamy, about 5 minutes. Stir the 2 cups flour and the 1 teaspoon salt together in a bowl. Add the yeast mixture, gradually working it in with your hands to make a slightly sticky dough. Knead briefly on a lightly floured board, dusting with flour as needed, then cover with an inverted bowl and let rest for 15 minutes. The bowl will create a warm environment for the dough to rise slightly.

Mix the onion, parsley, butter, spices, salt to taste, and cheese together in a bowl. For additional flavor, brown the chopped onion on the griddle or in the oven before mixing with the other filling ingredients.

Moisten your work surface and hands with olive oil and divide the dough into 8 equal portions. Shape each into a ball. Working with 1 ball at a time, flatten into a very thin square. If the dough is elastic and wants to spring back, let it rest for a few moments, then try again. The square should be as thin as you can make it without tearing. Spread some of the filling over the dough. Fold it in thirds like a letter. With a short side nearest you, fold the bottom third toward the center, then fold the top third under the center, accordion-style, to make a small square. Repeat with the remaining dough.

With oiled hands, pat and stretch each small square into a 5-inch square. You may use a rolling pin for this if you choose. The square should be as thin as you can make it without tearing the dough.

Preheat a cast-iron griddle to medium high heat in the oven or on the grill. Grease it lightly with oil. Place half of the flattened squares of dough on the griddle and cook on both sides until golden brown, about 2 minutes per side. Transfer to a wire rack and repeat to cook the remaining breads. Serve warm.

# Baguette Pain a l'Ancienne

Peter Reinhart is a well-known cookbook author; his *Crust and Crumb, The Bread Baker's Apprentice,* and *Whole Grain Breads* have been graced with prestigious awards. At Ramekins, where he occasionally teaches bread classes, Peter and I baked bread and pizzas together in the wood-fired oven after his last class. This recipe came from his *The Bread Baker's Apprentice.* It is an amazing formula that can be turned into baguettes, ciabatta, focaccia, and pizza. That baking session was about a lot more than the recipe. It was about the primary message of this book: joyfully cooking and sharing with others at the fire.

MAKES 6 BAGUETTES, 4 CIABATTA, 6 TO 8 PIZZAS, OR ONE 17 BY 12-INCH FOCACCIA

6$^1$/$_2$ cups unbleached bread flour, plus more for sprinkling

2$^1$/$_4$ teaspoons Kosher salt

1$^3$/$_4$ teaspoons instant yeast

2$^1$/$_4$ cups plus 2 tablespoons to 3 cups water,
   ice cold (40°F)

Semolina flour or cornmeal, for dusting

Combine 6 cups of the flour, salt, yeast, and 2¼ cups plus 2 tablespoons of water in the bowl of the electric mixer with the paddle attachment and mix for 2 minutes on low speed. Switch to the dough hook and mix for 5 to 6 minutes on medium speed. The dough should be sticky on the bottom of the bowl but it should release from the sides of the bowl. If not, sprinkle in a small amount of flour until this occurs (or dribble in water if the dough seems too stiff and clears the bottom as well as the sides of the bowl). Lightly oil a large bowl and immediately transfer the dough with a spatula or bowl scraper dipped in water into the bowl. Mist the top of the dough with spray oil and cover the bowl with plastic wrap.

Immediately place the bowl in the refrigerator and retard overnight.

The next day, check the dough to see if it has risen in the refrigerator. It will probably be partially risen but not doubled in size (the amount of rise will depend on how cold the refrigerator is and how often the door was opened). Leave the bowl of dough out at room temperature for 2 to 3 hours (or longer if necessary) to allow the dough to wake up, lose its chill, and continue fermenting.

When the dough has doubled from its original prerefrigerated size, liberally sprinkle the counter with bread flour (about ½ cup). Gently transfer the dough to the floured counter with a plastic dough scraper that has been dipped in cold water, dipping your hands as well to keep the dough from sticking to you. Try to degas the dough as little as possible as you transfer it. If the dough is very wet, sprinkle more flour over the top as well as under it. Dry your hands thoroughly and then dip them in flour. Roll the dough gently in the sprinkled flour to coat it thoroughly, simultaneously stretching it into an oblong about 8 inches long and 6 inches wide. If it is too sticky to handle, continue sprinkling flour over it. Dip a metal pastry scraper into cool water to keep it from sticking to the dough, and cut the dough in half widthwise with the pastry scraper by pressing it down through the dough until it severs it, then dipping it again in the water and repeating this action until you have cut down the full length of the dough. (Do not use this blade as a saw; use it as a pincer, pinching the dough cleanly with each cut.) Let the dough relax for 5 minutes.

Prepare a very hot fire (500°F) in a wood-fired oven (550°F if your oven goes this high). Cover the back of two 17 by 12-inch sheet pans with baking parchment and dust with semolina flour or cornmeal.

Take 1 of the dough pieces and repeat the cutting action with the pastry scraper, but this time cut off 3 equal-sized lengths. Then do the same with the remaining half. This should give you 6 lengths. Flour your hands and carefully lift 1 of the dough strips and transfer it to the parchment-lined pans, gently pulling it to the length of the pan or to the length of your baking stone. If it springs back, let it rest for 5 minutes and then gently pull it out again. Place 3 strips on the pan, and then repeat with the remaining strips and pan. Let sit at room temperature for 1 to 2 hours to proof.

Take 1 pan to the preheated oven and carefully slide the dough, parchment and all, onto the baking stone (depending on the direction of the stone, you may choose to slide the dough and parchment off the side of the sheet pan instead of off the end); or bake directly on the sheet pan. Make sure the pieces aren't touching (you can reach in and straighten the parchment or the dough strips if need be). Pour 1 cup hot water into the steam pan and close the door. After 30 seconds, spray the oven walls with water and close the door. Meanwhile, dust the other pan of strips with flour, mist with spray oil, and slip into a food-grade plastic bag or cover with a towel or plastic wrap. If you don't plan to bake these strips within 1 hour, refrigerate the pan and bake later or the next day.

The bread should begin to turn golden brown within 8 or 9 minutes. If the loaves are baking unevenly at this point, rotate them 180 degrees. Continue baking 10 to 15 minutes more, or until the bread is a rich golden brown and the internal temperature registers at least 205°F.

Transfer the hot breads to a cooling rack. They should feel very light, almost airy, and will cool in about 20 minutes. While these are cooling, you can bake the remaining loaves, remembering to remove the parchment from the oven and turn the oven up to 500°F or higher before baking the second round.

# Pita Bread

Though pita bread is made throughout the Middle East, we have come to identify it with Greece. When baking, it puffs up like a small balloon and then deflates when removed from the oven. This version has a bit of whole-wheat flour in it for extra nuttiness and added flavor. Make a batch or two ahead and freeze some to use later; these pita reheat easily. Try these filled with strips of roasted Mustard and Lemon Chicken (page 92) and topped with a dollop of Greek yogurt.

MAKES 12 PITA BREADS

2 cups warm water (105° to 115°F)

2 teaspoons honey

1½ teaspoons active dry yeast

4 cups all-purpose flour, plus more for kneading

½ cup whole-wheat flour

2 teaspoons Kosher salt

3 tablespoons olive oil, plus more for brushing

Place ½ cup of the water in a small bowl and stir in the honey to dissolve. Sprinkle the yeast over the top and stir until the yeast is dissolved. Let stand until foamy, about 5 minutes.

In a stand mixer fitted with the dough hook, mix the flours, salt, and the 3 tablespoons olive oil together. With the mixer on low speed, add the yeast mixture, then gradually add the remaining 1½ cups water and mix until the flour is completely integrated. Knead dough on a lightly floured board for about 5 minutes, or until smooth, elastic, and no longer sticky, dusting with flour as needed. Place the dough in an oiled bowl and oil the top of the dough lightly, then turn the dough to coat it with oil. Cover with a damp towel or plastic wrap and let rise in a warm place until doubled in size, about 1 hour.

Prepare a very hot fire (500°F) in a wood-fired oven or cooker, or prepare a hot indirect fire in a wood-fired grill. If using a conventional oven, place the oven rack in the lowest position.

Turn the dough out on a lightly floured board and knead to remove the air bubbles. Roll into a log and divide the dough evenly into 12 pieces. Form each piece of dough into a ball, and then use a rolling pin to flatten into disks about ¼ inch thick and 6 inches in diameter. Place the disks on a lightly greased baking sheet and let rise, uncovered, until almost doubled in thickness, 30 to 45 minutes.

Bake on the baking sheet or grill over indirect heat until puffed and lightly golden, 5 to 10 minutes. Remove from the heat and let cool on wire racks for 5 minutes.

Cut each pita into a half circle and separate on the cut line with a fork to create a pocket.

# Turkish Spicy Meat-Filled Flatbread

These stuffed flatbreads are shaped much like meat-filled galettes. Lamb is the meat of choice in many Mediterranean cuisines, and here it is combined with other key ingredients of the region—eggplant and pomegranate—along with the warm aromatics often used in Turkish cuisine.

MAKES 4 FLATBREADS

DOUGH

1/2 teaspoon active dry yeast

1/2 cup warm water (105° to 115°F)

1 3/4 cups all-purpose flour, plus more for kneading

1/4 teaspoon kosher salt

1 tablespoon olive oil

FILLING

2 tablespoons olive oil, plus more for sautéing

1 yellow onion, finely chopped

1 small unpeeled globe eggplant, cut into small dice

1/2 teaspoon kosher salt, plus more for sprinkling

1/2 pound lean ground lamb

2 tablespoons pomegranate molasses

1 large tomato, peeled and diced

1/4 teaspoon ground allspice

1/2 teaspoon ground cinnamon

1/4 teaspoon freshly ground black pepper

2 tablespoons pine nuts, toasted

1 tablespoon freshly squeezed lemon juice, or as needed

Prepare a hot fire (475°F) in a wood-fired oven.

To make the dough, sprinkle the yeast over 1/4 cup warm water in a small bowl and stir to dissolve the yeast. Let stand until foamy, about 5 minutes. Combine the flour and salt in a large bowl. Drizzle in the olive oil and combine using your hands or a stand mixer. Add the yeast mixture plus the remaining water. Knead for 5 minutes using a dough hook or by hand on a floured board (adding flour if needed when kneading by hand) until the dough is smooth and elastic, 5 to 7 minutes. Place the dough in an oiled bowl and turn to coat it with oil. Cover with a damp towel or plastic wrap and let rise in a warm place for 30 minutes, until doubled in size.

To make the filling, toss the olive oil, onion, and eggplant together and sprinkle with salt. Spread on a baking sheet. Place on the floor of the oven and cook until the eggplant is soft, about 7 minutes. Stir in the 1/2 teaspoon salt. In a small cast-iron skillet in the oven, sauté the lamb in a small amount of olive oil and cook until brown, about 5 minutes. Discard any fat. Remove from the heat and stir in the pomegranate molasses, tomato, spices, and pine nuts. Add lemon juice to taste.

Divide the dough into 4 equal pieces on a floured board and roll into balls. Flatten each ball into a 5-inch disk. Stretch the dough into a thin disk about 6 inches across. Place on a parchment-lined baking sheet. Place one-fourth of the meat filling in the center of each disk and spread to about 1 1/2 inches from the edge. In 4 to 5 increments, fold the dough up toward the center to contain the filling. Lightly brush with olive oil and lightly dust with salt.

Place the baking sheet in the oven and bake for 12 to 15 minutes, or until beautifully golden. Let cool for 5 minutes, then serve hot.

# Spanish Coca with Smoky Romesco and Potatoes

Coca is the Spanish version of pizza. Here, it is spread with my Smoky Romesco Sauce, a basic in the Spanish pantry. When topped with green onions, roasted potatoes, and sliced hard-cooked eggs, it is an edible canvas of the sunny colors and flavors of this part of the Mediterranean.

MAKES ONE 9 BY 14-INCH FLATBREAD

DOUGH

2¹/₂ teaspoons active dry yeast

³/₄ cup warm water (105° to 115°F)

1³/₄ cups unbleached all-purpose flour, plus more
    for kneading

³/₄ teaspoon kosher salt

1 tablespoon olive oil

TOPPING

¹/₄ cup olive oil, plus more for brushing

1¹/₂ teaspoons sweet pimentón (Spanish smoked paprika)

¹/₂ teaspoon kosher salt

¹/₄ teaspoon freshly ground black pepper

¹/₂ cup Smoky Romesco Sauce (page 188)

8 green onions, trimmed to light green area and
    cut into ¹/₄-inch slices

1 tablespoon whole fresh oregano leaves

2 large Yukon Gold potatoes, cubed and roasted

2 hard-cooked eggs, sliced into rounds

To make the dough, sprinkle the yeast over ¹/₄ cup of the water and stir to dissolve. Let stand until foamy, about 5 minutes, or until dissolved. Sift the 1³/₄ cups flour and the salt onto a work surface and make a well in the center. Add the yeast mixture, remaining water, and the olive oil. Mix the ingredients in the well together with your fingertips, then gradually draw in flour to make a dough. Knead, dusting with flour as necessary, for 5 to 10 minutes, or until elastic. The dough should be soft, but only slightly sticky. Transfer the dough to an oiled bowl and turn to coat it with oil. Cover with a damp towel or plastic wrap and let rise in a warm place until doubled in bulk, 45 minutes to 1 hour.

Prepare a very hot fire (525° to 550°F) in a wood-fired oven or cooker.

Knead the dough lightly on a floured board for 2 minutes. Roll into a 9 by 14-inch rectangle, stretching to size with your hands. It should be about ¹/₂ inch thick. Transfer to an oiled baking sheet and dimple the surface of the dough with your fingertips so it does not puff evenly.

To make the topping, mix the ¹/₄ cup olive oil, pimentón, salt, and pepper together in a small bowl and brush half of this mixture generously on the dough. Spread evenly with the romesco sauce, then the green onions and oregano. Brush the edges of the crust with olive oil. Leave in a warm place for 10 to 15 minutes, or until the dough is puffy.

Bake the bread in the oven for 10 minutes, rotating the pan once to bake evenly. Top with the roasted potatoes and continue to bake until the crust is brown and crisp, about 15 minutes. Remove from the oven and brush the edges of the crust with olive oil. Top with sliced eggs and cut into serving-size slices or squares. Serve warm or at room temperature.

# CHAPTER 5

# Wood-Fired Grilling

The most popular form of cooking in the world must be grilling. Cooking simple dishes over live fire can be fast, fun, and easy, and grilling over wood raises fast food to new levels of flavors. This chapter covers grilling from an eclectic assortment of global cuisines. The recipes include pizzas, flatbreads, simple steaks, stuffed and rubbed meats, skewered and planked seafood, marinated meat and poultry, and grilled salads, while the grilling methods include the use of wood-fired grills, ovens, fireplaces, fire pits, and campfires.

Because grilling involves cooking over high heat, food needs at least one of these layers of protection to keep it from drying out: (1) a layer of fat; (2) a leaf wrap; (3) a crust or a dry rub; (4) a skin or husk; (5) a marinade and frequent mopping.

Make a big fire and let it die down before cooking. Don't rush into grilling as soon as the flames start dancing. Be patient and wait for hot coals.

# Grilled Cilantro-Mint Naan

Jerry Traunfeld was the executive chef for many years at the HerbFarm in Woodinville, Washington, near Seattle and now owns Seattle's Poppy Restaurant. Jerry's finely tuned palate served him well in the development of an expansive herb-focused menu at the award-winning restaurant. Jerry's version of naan, a simple flatbread from India by way of Afghanistan, was created for this book. Filled with a combination of flavor-packed herbs and richly flavored cashews, it's wonderful!

MAKES 10 BREADS

DOUGH

5 cups unbleached all-purpose flour

2 teaspoons sugar

4 teaspoons baking powder

4 teaspoons kosher salt

1 large egg

1/2 cup whole-milk yogurt

1 1/4 cups warm water (105° to 115°F)

1/4 cup peanut oil or canola oil

FILLING

1/2 cup fresh mint leaves

1 1/2 cups coarsely chopped fresh cilantro

1 clove garlic, chopped

1 tablespoon chopped fresh ginger

1/4 cup raw cashews

1 teaspoon kosher salt

6 tablespoons peanut oil or canola oil

4 ounces clarified butter, for brushing

To make the dough, combine the flour, sugar, baking powder, and salt in the bowl of an electric mixer fitted with a paddle attachment and mix together. Whisk the egg and yogurt in a bowl, then whisk in the water and oil. Pour the liquid ingredients into the dry ingredients. Using the dough hook, knead the dough for about 5 minutes. Turn the dough out onto a floured board, form it into a ball, and divide it into 10 equal pieces. Form each piece into a ball, place on a baking sheet lined with parchment paper, cover with plastic wrap, and rest for at least 1 hour or up to 1 1/2 hours.

Prepare a medium-hot fire (450°F) in a wood-fired grill.

To make the filling, combine the mint, cilantro, garlic, ginger, cashews, and salt in a food processor. Process until finely chopped. Scrape down the sides, turn the machine back on, and pour in the oil. Scoop the filling into a small bowl.

On a floured board, roll a ball of dough into a 6-inch circle. Spread the center with about 2 teaspoons of the filling. Gather the edges up, pinching them together in the center, to seal in the filling. Turn the dough over and gently roll it into a 7-inch circle. Transfer to a parchment-lined baking sheet. Continue forming the dough, layering parchment in between the breads if you stack them.

Place about 3 breads directly on the grate. Cook for 1 to 2 minutes, until the breads look puffy and are lightly browned on the bottom. Turn the breads over and finish cooking the other side. Brush lightly with clarified butter. Continue to cook the remaining breads. Serve warm, whole or cut in half.

# Tuscan Grilled Pizza with Escarole

Cookbook author Joanne Weir is known for her flavor-packed Mediterranean-inspired food. Her book *From Tapas to Meze* shows the breadth of her Mediterranean influences. Here, Joanne shares a favorite pizza recipe that we adapted for grilling using a Tuscan grill that fits into the fireplace of her home in San Francisco. The bitter escarole on this pizza is balanced by the sweet pine nuts, creamy cheeses, and the salty olives. The dough for a grilled pizza needs a bit more structure from gluten to keep it from oozing through the grates of the grill, which is why this one is kneaded for a longer time than other pizza doughs.

MAKES TWO 10- TO 11-INCH PIZZAS

2 cloves garlic, minced

4 tablespoons extra-virgin olive oil, plus more for brushing

$3/4$ cup shredded mozzarella cheese

$3/4$ cup shredded Italian fontina cheese

$1/4$ cup pine nuts

Leaves from 1 head escarole, cut into 1-inch-wide strips

2 teaspoons balsamic vinegar

Pinch of red pepper flakes

Salt and freshly ground black pepper

Joanne Weir's Pizza Dough (recipe follows)

$1/2$ cup pitted niçoise olives, coarsely chopped

Prepare a hot fire (475° to 500°F) in a wood-fired grill.

Combine the garlic and 2 tablespoons of the olive oil in a small bowl and let stand for 30 minutes. Combine the mozzarella and fontina in a bowl.

Heat a large skillet on the grill, add the pine nuts, and toast, stirring occasionally, until golden, 1 to 2 minutes. Remove from the pan and set aside.

Heat the remaining 2 tablespoons olive oil in the same pan over medium heat. Add the escarole and cook, stirring occasionally until it wilts, 1 to 2 minutes. Add the vinegar and red pepper flakes. Season to taste with salt and pepper. Set aside

Divide the dough into 2 round pieces and form each into a ball. Do not work the dough too much. Roll one ball into a 10- to 11-inch round. Transfer to a lightly oiled baking sheet and brush the top of the dough with olive oil. Repeat with the second ball of dough.

Take the dough and all of the toppings to the grill. Place one pizza round, oiled side down, on the grill. Cover the grill and cook for 5 minutes. Turn the pizza over and brush the marked side to within ½ inch of the edge with the garlic-infused oil. Move the pizza off direct heat. Sprinkle half of the combined cheeses on top of the oil. Top with half of the escarole, pine nuts, and olives, spreading evenly. Close the lid and bake until golden and crisp, about 7 minutes. Repeat with the remaining ingredients to make a second pizza.

## JOANNE WEIR'S PIZZA DOUGH

### MAKES ENOUGH DOUGH FOR TWO 10- TO 11-INCH PIZZAS

2 teaspoons active dry yeast
¾ cup plus 2 tablespoons warm water (105° to 115°F)
2 cups unbleached bread flour
1 tablespoon extra-virgin olive oil
½ teaspoon salt

In a bowl, combine the yeast, ¼ cup of the warm water, and ¼ cup of the flour in a small bowl. Let stand for 30 minutes. Add the remaining 1¾ cups flour, ½ cup plus 2 tablespoons warm water, the olive oil, and salt. Mix the dough thoroughly. Turn out onto a floured board and knead until smooth, elastic and a bit tacky to the touch, 7 to 8 minutes. Place in an oiled bowl and turn to cover with oil. Cover with a damp towel or plastic wrap and let rise in a warm place until doubled in volume, 1 to 1½ hours. Or, let the dough rise in the refrigerator overnight. The next day, bring the dough to room temperature.

# Grilled Flank Steak with Red Peppers and Fontina Cheese

Italian cuisine often features stuffed and rolled meat or fish. This recipe uses inexpensive yet flavorful flank steak. Pounded chicken or turkey breast, pork loin, or fish can be substituted. The grilled rolls are sliced into beautiful spirals and serve with gremolata reserved from the stuffing and a wonderful wood-roasted wine sauce.

**SERVES 6 AS A MAIN COURSE**

1 (1½- to 2-pound) flank steak
Kosher salt and freshly ground black pepper

GREMOLATA STUFFING
1 cup coarsely chopped fresh flat-leaf parsley
¼ cup julienned fresh basil
6 cloves garlic, blanched and minced (page 192)
Grated zest of 1 lemon
⅓ cup bread crumbs or panko (Japanese bread crumbs)
½ teaspoon red pepper flakes
½ teaspoon kosher salt
2 tablespoons olive oil, for moistening

2 red bell peppers, roasted and peeled (page 191)
2 cups packed spinach leaves
8 ounces Italian fontina or Monterey Jack cheese,
    thinly sliced
Olive oil, for brushing
Wood-Roasted Red Pepper Wine Sauce (page 191)

Prepare a hot fire (475° to 500°F) in a wood-fired oven or grill.

Butterfly the steak by slicing through it horizontally (with the grain), cutting almost through, leaving halves attached by ½ inch. Open and flatten the cut meat and lightly season with salt and pepper. Pound the steak to create a fairly even thickness. Set aside.

To make the gremolata stuffing, combine all the ingredients in a bowl. Set aside, reserving 3 tablespoons for garnish.

Cut the roasted red peppers into 4 large slabs. Lay the spinach leaves over the opened steak. Line with cheese slices, then the red pepper slabs. Sprinkle with the gremolata stuffing. Roll up the steak tightly lengthwise. Tie the rolled steak with kitchen string about every 3 inches. Brush with olive oil and season lightly with salt and pepper.

Place the meat on a grate in the oven or on the grill and turn to brown on all sides, about 10 minutes. Move off direct heat and continue cooking for 20 to 25 minutes, or until an instant-read thermometer inserted in the center registers 120° to 130°F. Transfer to a carving board, tent loosely with aluminum foil, and let rest for 10 minutes, or until an instant-read thermometer inserted in the center registers 130° to 135°F. Cut into ½-inch-thick rounds, sprinkle with the reserved gremolata, and serve with the wine sauce.

# Grilled Pork Loin Stuffed with Chard, Fennel, and Olives

The Swiss chard in this dish has a slightly bitter flavor that works well with the fragrant fennel and salty olives. The sliced meat is topped with a delicious uncooked Italian sauce thickened with leftover bread and pulverized toasted nuts.

## SERVES 6 AS A MAIN COURSE

BRINE

1/3 cup salt

1/3 cup sugar

4 cups water, at room temperature

1 (3-pound) pork loin, boned

STUFFING

4 to 6 large Swiss chard leaves, stemmed

1/4 cup olive oil, plus more for brushing

1 pound green garlic or leeks, trimmed and sliced
     lengthwise

1 medium fennel bulb, thinly sliced and chopped

1 cup picholine olives, pitted and finely chopped

1 cup dry white wine

Grated zest of 1 orange

1/2 cup chopped fresh flat-leaf parsley

2 teaspoons fennel seed

Kosher salt and freshly ground white pepper

Olive oil, for brushing

Toasted Walnut Sauce (recipe follows)

Prepare a hot fire (450°F) in a wood-fired grill.

To make the brine, dissolve the salt and sugar in the water. Add the pork loin to the brine and refrigerate for 2 to 3 hours. Rinse the pork loin, pat dry with paper towels, and allow to come to room temperature.

To make the stuffing, blanch the chard leaves in salted water for 1 minute, then immediately place in a bowl of ice water. Drain and dry the leaves on paper towels. Heat the 1/4 cup olive oil in a sauté pan over medium heat and add the green garlic. Cook until soft, about 5 minutes, then add the fennel bulb and cook until the fennel is soft, about 7 minutes. Add the olives and wine. Cook until the wine is almost evaporated. Add the orange zest, parsley, fennel seed, and salt and pepper to taste. Set aside.

Unroll the pork and trim off any fat. Slice the pork into thirds lengthwise, cutting to about 1/2 inch from all the way through. Open and lay the pork flat. Place plastic wrap over the pork and, using a flat meat pounder or small skillet, flatten to any even thickness of about 1/2 inch. Season lightly with salt and pepper. Lay the blanched chard leaves over the pork to create a lining. Spread the fennel stuffing mixture over the chard to within 1/2 inch of the edges. Roll the pork up jelly-roll style, starting with one long side, and secure every 2 inches with kitchen string.

Lightly brush with olive oil and season well with salt and pepper. Place the pork on the grill and rotate until all sides are golden and lightly crisp, about 10 minutes. Move the roast to the side of the grill, away from direct heat. Cover and cook, turning the meat every 5 minutes or so, for 20 minutes, or until the roast is evenly golden and an instant-read thermometer inserted into the meat (not the stuffing) registers 145°F. Transfer the meat to a carving board, tent loosely with aluminum foil, and let rest for 15 minutes. Remove the strings and cut the meat into ½-inch-thick rounds. Serve topped with the walnut sauce.

## TOASTED WALNUT SAUCE

### MAKES ABOUT 4 CUPS

2 slices day-old white artisan bread, such as pugliese, levain, sweet baguette

2 to 3 cups whole milk

2 cups (8 ounces) walnut halves or pieces, toasted

4 cloves roasted garlic (page 192)

1 tablespoon fresh thyme leaves

Kosher salt and freshly ground white pepper

1/3 cup olive oil

Red pepper flakes (optional)

Soak the bread in enough milk to cover. Add the mixture to a food processor along with the walnuts, garlic, and thyme. Pulse into a paste. Add salt and white pepper to taste. With the machine running, add the olive oil. Add milk as necessary to achieve a sauce-like consistency. Add red pepper flakes to taste. Use now, or cover and refrigerate for up to 1 week.

# Mediterranean Lamb Kebabs with Pomegranate Glaze

Lamb, pomegranate, and apricots is a classic Mediterranean combination. Pomegranate molasses, which is sometimes called pomegranate concentrate, is a pantry staple in parts of the Mediterranean. It serves as a meat tenderizer as well as a flavor enhancer. Look for it in specialty foods stores, or online (see Resources). Serve this dish with a rice pilaf or couscous. Note: you will need 16 wooden skewers for this recipe.

SERVES 8 AS A MAIN COURSE

MARINADE

1/2 cup chopped onion

4 cloves garlic, chopped

1 1/2 teaspoons ground cumin

2 teaspoons sweet Hungarian paprika

1/2 teaspoon chopped fresh ginger

1 teaspoon freshly ground black pepper

2 tablespoons pomegranate molasses or concentrate

1 tablespoon tomato paste

2 tablespoons olive oil

3 pounds boneless lamb shoulder, trimmed and cut
    into 1-inch cubes

24 bay leaves

36 dried Turkish apricot halves, soaked in warm water
    for 10 minutes

Kosher salt

1/4 cup chopped pistachio nuts

To make the marinade, puree the onion, garlic, cumin, paprika, ginger, and pepper in a blender. Add the pomegranate molasses and tomato paste, then pulse until blended. With the machine running, drizzle in the olive oil until blended.

Put the lamb in a shallow dish, coat with half of the marinade, and let stand at room temperature for 2 hours or refrigerate overnight. Reserve the remaining marinade to use as a grilling glaze.

Prepare a hot fire (450°F) in a wood-fired grill.

Remove the lamb from the refrigerator 30 minutes before cooking. Soak 16 wooden skewers in water for 30 minutes. Thread the lamb, bay leaves, and apricot halves alternately on the skewers. Lightly salt the lamb. In a small saucepan, bring the reserved marinade to a boil and cook for 5 minutes.

Grill the skewers for about 4 minutes on each side for medium-rare. Brush with marinade while grilling and again after removing from the heat. Arrange the skewers on a platter and sprinkle with the pistachios.

# Grilled Duck Breasts with Lavender-Herb Rub

A rich, fragrant dish, these duck breasts are perfumed with the aromatics of southwest France, then grilled to crisp the fatty skin. Served sliced and fanned over tender baby greens lightly dressed with citrus vinaigrette, this is a wonderful dish to serve as a first course or as a light main course.

**SERVES 6 AS A MAIN COURSE**

2 tablespoons herbes de Provence

2 tablespoons fresh or dried lavender buds

1 tablespoon coriander seeds

1 teaspoon fennel seeds

1/2 teaspoon cracked black peppercorns

Grated zest of 1 orange

2 (1-pound) Muscovy duck breasts

Kosher salt

6 tablespoons olive oil

3 tablespoons freshly squeezed orange juice

Freshly ground white pepper

3 cups baby greens

Put the herbs and spices in a spice grinder and spin until very finely ground. In a small bowl, combine the orange zest and the ground herbs and spices.

Cutting only through the skin and fat, score the duck breasts with 5 diagonal lines about 1 inch apart, cutting just deep enough to slice the skin but not the flesh. Rub both sides of the duck breast with the herb mixtures, spreading it evenly and working some into the score marks on the skin side. Use now, or wrap in plastic wrap and refrigerate for up to 1 day, which will improve the flavors.

Prepare a hot fire (450° to 475°F) in a wood-fired grill. If refrigerated, remove the duck and let stand at room temperature for 30 minutes before cooking. Lightly salt the duck breasts.

Grill the duck over direct heat, skin sides down, for 3 minutes, until just caramelized. Have a water sprayer handy to reduce possible flare-ups from the duck fat. Transfer, skin sides down, to a cast-iron skillet. Place to the side of the grill, away from direct heat, and cook for 8 minutes, or until very rare. Drain off any duck fat and turn the breasts over. Cook for 3 to 4 minutes for medium-rare. Remove from the heat, loosely tent with aluminum foil, and let rest for 5 minutes. Transfer to a carving board and cut on the diagonal into 1/4-inch-thick slices.

Whisk the olive oil into the orange juice in a small bowl and add salt and pepper to taste. Just before serving, toss the baby greens in the vinaigrette and divide among 6 plates. Top each with 3 slices of duck. Drizzle the duck with any remaining vinaigrette.

# Tandoori Chicken

Tandoori chicken is easily identified by its red color and is named for the oven it's cooked in. The tandoor is a cylindrical clay or ceramic oven heated to temperatures of 550° to 750°F or more. Meat and vegetables are skewered, then lowered into the oven. The high heat creates a crisp crust and leaves the meat moist. For the best flavor, marinate overnight. The red food coloring is optional.

This recipe is adapted to a grill or Big Green Egg ceramic cooker, which is the next best thing to an actual tandoor oven.

SERVES 8 AS A MAIN COURSE

4 chicken thighs

4 chicken breasts

MARINADE

1 cup nonfat yogurt, drained through a fine-mesh sieve
      for 1 hour

Juice of 2 lemons

4 drops of red food coloring (optional)

4 cloves garlic, minced

1-inch piece fresh ginger, minced

2 teaspoons garam masala

2 teaspoons ground cumin

$1/2$ teaspoon cayenne pepper

Kosher salt

4 small lemons, plus lemon wedges for garnish

Prepare a hot fire (500°F). If using a Big Green Egg, wood-fired oven, or other kettle-shaped grill, place a 6-inch-deep high-fired ceramic flower pot with a 5- to 6-inch base upside down in the bottom of the cooker. Surround the pot with charcoal 3 inches deep; mesquite charcoal is preferable because it burns very hot.

Remove the skin from the chicken, rinse, and pat dry. Cut a few $1/2$-inch-deep slashes in the chicken. Cut the breasts in half so that they are similar in size to the thighs.

To make the marinade, combine all the ingredients in a large bowl. Add the chicken, turning to coat it. Cover and refrigerate for at least 4 hours or preferably overnight.

Remove the chicken from the marinade and place in a strainer or colander to drain for 1 hour.

Skewer 3 to 4 pieces of chicken about 2 inches from the top of the skewer and end with a lemon to hold the chicken in place. Repeat to skewer all the chicken. Using a fire poker, spread apart the hot coals slightly. Place the pointed ends of the skewers into the drain hole of the inverted pot, keeping the chicken free from the sides of the oven and exposed to the radiant heat. Cover and cook for 10 minutes, then rotate the skewers to cook the chicken evenly. Cover and cook for 15 minutes, or until the chicken is cooked through. Remove the skewers from the cooker and let stand for 5 minutes. Serve with lemon wedges.

# Plank-Roasted Pacific Salmon

This recipe from award-winning cookbook author John Ash features plank roasting, an old technique used by the Northwest Indians who tied or nailed salmon to cedar or alder planks and tilted them over an open fire to cook. The cure in this recipe flavors the fish and acts as a brine to keep it moist.

### SERVES 8 AS A MAIN COURSE

CURE
2 tablespoons kosher salt
1/4 cup sugar
2 teaspoons coriander seeds
2 teaspoons fennel seeds
15 black peppercorns
3 bay leaves
2 cups dry white wine
1/3 cup snipped fresh dill

8 4-ounce or 2 1-pound salmon fillets, skin on and
    pin bones removed
Olive oil, for brushing

Soak two 12 by 7-inch, 5/8-inch-thick oak planks in water for 2 hours.

To make the cure, combine the salt, sugar, coriander and fennel seeds, peppercorns, bay leaves, and wine in a nonreactive saucepan. Bring to a boil, decrease the heat to a simmer, and cook for 2 minutes. Remove from the heat, add the dill, and let cool completely. Use now, or cover and refrigerate for up to 1 week.

Put the salmon fillets in a baking dish large enough to hold them in a single layer. Pour the cooled cure over the fish and let stand for 15 to 30 minutes, turning once or twice. Remove the salmon from the cure and drain. It is fine if some of the spices or dill adheres to the salmon. Lightly brush the salmon with olive oil.

Prepare a medium heat fire (400°F) in a wood-fired grill. Have a spray bottle of water ready to extinguish flare-ups. Place the soaked planks on the grill and close the lid. Heat until the planks begin to smoke and crackle a bit, about 3 minutes. Flip the planks over, then place the salmon, skin side down, on the marked side of the planks. Cover and grill until the salmon is just cooked through and slightly translucent in the center, about 6 minutes.

Transfer the plank with the salmon to a heatproof platter, or transfer the salmon to a warmed platter or plates. Serve hot or at room temperature.

# Fennel-Rubbed Halibut with Fava Bean Ragout

This combination of sweet, succulent halibut and spring vegetables in a golden saffron broth is visually seductive, while the earthy fragrance of saffron, favas, and mushrooms is intoxicating! Paula Wolfert's easy method of preparing fava beans makes this dish much easier to prepare.

SERVES 6 AS A MAIN COURSE

1/4 cup ground fennel seeds

1/3 cup olive oil

1/2 teaspoon kosher salt

1/4 teaspoon freshly ground white pepper

6 (6-ounce) halibut fillets, skinned

RAGOUT

1 cup dry white wine

1 cup vegetable or chicken stock or broth

1/2 teaspoon saffron threads

4 tablespoons unsalted butter

2 tablespoons minced shallots

4 small young leeks (white part only), well rinsed and
    sliced crosswise (see note on opposite page)

1 pound chanterelle mushrooms, cut into bite-sized pieces

5 sprigs thyme

1 pound fava beans, steamed and shelled
    (see opposite page)

1 pound baby carrots, blanched

1/2 cup fresh flat-leaf parsley leaves

Kosher salt and freshly ground white pepper

Prepare a medium-hot fire (450°F) in a wood-fired grill.

Combine the fennel seeds and olive oil to create a paste. Add the salt and pepper. Rub each fillet with the mixture and set aside at room temperature.

To make the ragout, bring the white wine and stock to a low boil in a small nonreactive saucepan. Add the saffron threads, remove from the heat, and set aside.

Melt 2 tablespoons of the butter in a large sauté pan over medium heat. Add the shallots and sauté until soft, about 3 minutes, then add the leeks and mushrooms and sauté for 5 minutes. Add the thyme sprigs. Add the saffron liquid and stir to scrape up the browned bits from the bottom of the pan. Stir in the remaining 2 tablespoons butter, the fava beans, and carrots and cook over low heat for 5 to 7 minutes, until the favas and carrots are tender. Remove the thyme and add the parsley. Season to taste with salt and pepper. Set aside and keep warm.

Oil the grill grids and add the halibut. Cover and cook on one side until the flesh is opaque throughout, 8 to 10 minutes. (With the lid closed, the delicate halibut does not need to be turned over and cooked on both sides.) Transfer to a warmed platter, grilled side up, surround with the ragout, and serve.

CLEANING LEEKS

Leeks add an incredible depth of flavor to home-made soups, but they are like sand traps. Trim off the root ends, then make two perpendicular cuts down the entire length of the dark green leaves. Swish the leeks in a bowl of warm water (I find that cold water makes the sand cling), separating the dark green leaves to expose any sand. Then chop them and swish around in a fresh bowl of water. Lift out chopped leeks with your fingers, allowing any sediment to sink to the bottom of the bowl

## Steaming Fava Beans

Rather than the tedious three-step method of shelling, blanching, and peeling fava beans, try this time-saver from Paula Wolfert.

Place unshelled fava beans in a steamer rack over boiling water; cover and cook until wilted, about 15 minutes. Remove from the steamer and let cool to the touch. Remove the pods, then remove the skin from each fava bean.

If the beans will be cooked further, cut back a bit on the steaming time so the beans will be slightly undercooked when skinned.

# Grilled Shrimp with Herb Vinaigrette

This is a dish you can make with little preparation or cooking time. Anyone can be a successful shrimp griller. The key things to remember are: (1) brine the shrimp to assure moistness; (2) grill them with the shells on; (3) don't overcook them. The brightly flavored vinaigrette can be served with any other grilled fish or even chicken.

SERVES 6 AS FIRST COURSE

BRINE
1/3 cup salt
1/3 cup sugar
4 cups water, at room temperature

1 pound extra-large shrimp (16 to 20 count), shell on, scored down the back and deveined

MARINADE
4 cloves garlic, minced
Grated zest of 1 lime
1/2 teaspoon red pepper flakes
1/4 cup dry white wine
Juice of 2 limes
1/4 cup olive oil

6 handfuls baby arugula
Herb Vinaigrette (recipe follows)

To make the brine, dissolve the salt and sugar in the water. Add the shrimp and let stand for 20 to 30 minutes. Drain.

Prepare a medium-hot fire (450°F) in a wood-fired grill. Soak 6 wooden skewers in water for 30 minutes.

To make the marinade, whisk all the ingredients together in a large bowl. Toss with the shrimp. Cover and refrigerate for 30 minutes.

Thread 3 shrimp on each skewer, piercing each through both ends. Let stand at room temperature for 15 minutes.

Grill for 1 to 2 minutes on each side, or until they just turn evenly pink. Serve on a bed of baby arugula and drizzle with the vinaigrette. Serve the remaining vinaigrette alongside for dipping.

## HERB VINAIGRETTE

MAKES ABOUT 2 CUPS

4 cloves garlic, blanched or poached (see page 192)
1 cup packed fresh flat-leaf parsley
1/4 cup fresh basil leaves
1/4 cup fresh mint leaves
1 teaspoon kosher salt
1/4 cup freshly squeezed lime juice
2 tablespoons mirin (Japanese cooking wine)
3/4 cup olive oil
1 teaspoon honey, or as needed

Combine all the ingredients except the olive oil and honey in a food processor or blender. With the machine running, gradually add the olive oil to create an emulsion. Add honey to taste. Taste and adjust the seasoning.

# Grilled Panzanella with Heirloom Tomatoes

Panzanella is a rustic Italian bread salad, created to use leftover bread. The vibrant tomatoes add moisture to the stale bread for a great summer main course or side dish. In this version, the bread is grilled for extra flavor. If your tomatoes are not at the peak of flavor, grill them, cut side down, until marked to bring out their natural sugars. Cut them into chunks and toss in the dressing before adding to the salad.

SERVES 6 TO 8 AS A FIRST COURSE

1 (1-pound) loaf day-old rustic bread, such as pugliese
    or ciabatta

6 cloves roasted garlic (page 192)

1/2 teaspoon coarse sea salt

3 tablespoons extra-virgin olive oil, plus more for brushing

DRESSING

1/3 cup Champagne or white balsamic vinegar

1/2 teaspoon sweet pimentón (Spanish smoked paprika)

3/4 cup extra-virgin olive oil

Sea salt

1 red bell pepper, roasted, peeled, and torn into
    narrow strips

4 green onions, finely chopped (including half of greens)

8 ounces haricots verts or baby Blue Lake green beans,
    blanched, drained, and cut into julienne

8 ounces tomatoes in mixed colors, cut into
    bite-sized pieces

3 lemon or English cucumbers, cut into small wedges

1/3 cup black oil-cured olives, pitted

3 tablespoons capers, rinsed and drained

Kosher salt and freshly ground black pepper

1 dozen fresh basil leaves, torn into bite-sized pieces

4 ounces Parmesan cheese, cut into thin shavings

Prepare a medium-hot fire (450°F) in a wood-fired grill, or plan to use a grill pan.

Trim the heel ends from the loaf and cut the bread into 1-inch slices. Mash the garlic and sea salt into a paste. Blend with 3 tablespoons of the olive oil. Brush one side of the bread slices with the garlic mixture.

Preheat a grill pan over medium-high heat, if using. Oil the grill grids or grill pan and toast the bread, dry side down, until lightly charred, about 3 minutes. Turn the bread over and repeat on the second side. Remove from the heat and let cool slightly. Tear the bread into bite-sized pieces and place in a large bowl.

To make the dressing, combine the vinegar and pimentón in a small bowl and gradually whisk in the oil to create an emulsion. Add salt to taste and set aside.

Combine the red pepper, green onions, beans, tomatoes, cucumbers, olives, and capers in a bowl. Lightly dress and add salt and pepper to taste. Let stand for 30 minutes, then add to the bread and toss. Add more dressing as needed to coat the bread. Add the basil leaves and toss again. Serve on a platter or on individual dishes, topped with Parmesan cheese.

# Salade Niçoise with Spring Vegetables

Salade niçoise is traditionally a composition of tender seasonal lettuces, green beans, baby potatoes, olives, and the best-quality tuna packed in olive oil. This version features tuna steaks grilled perfectly, then broken into chunks. You can substitute your favorite seasonal vegetables if you choose. This salad should not be chilled.

**SERVES 6 AS A MAIN COURSE**

DRESSING

1/4 cup Champagne vinegar

2 tablespoons minced shallots

2 teaspoons Dijon mustard

2 cloves roasted garlic (page 192), mashed into paste

1/2 teaspoon anchovy paste (optional)

1 cup olive oil

2 teaspoons fresh thyme leaves

1/4 cup minced fresh tarragon

Kosher salt and freshly ground black pepper

12 ounces haricots verts or baby Blue Lake green beans, trimmed

1/2 pound baby carrots, tops removed

1 1/2 pounds unpeeled baby red or yellow potatoes

1 1/2 pounds 1-inch-thick ahi tuna steaks

Olive oil, for brushing

Salt and freshly ground black pepper

8 cups young lettuce (butter, red oak, or spinach), torn into large pieces

1 pint cherry tomatoes, halved

1/2 cup niçoise or other small brine-cured black olives

3 hard-cooked eggs, quartered

3 tablespoons minced fresh flat-leaf parsley

1/4 cup capers, drained and rinsed

Prepare a medium-hot fire (450°F) in a wood-fired grill, or plan to use a grill pan.

To make the dressing, whisk the vinegar, shallots, mustard, garlic paste, and anchovy paste together in a small bowl until well combined. Gradually whisk in the oil until the mixture is emulsified. Whisk in the thyme, tarragon, and salt and pepper to taste. Set aside.

Cook the beans in a large pot of salted boiling water for 3 to 4 minutes, or until crisp-tender. Immediately transfer them to a bowl of ice water to stop the cooking. Remove when cooled, then drain and pat dry and set aside. Cook the carrots by the same method. Add the potatoes to salted boiling water and simmer, uncovered, until tender (15 to 20 minutes) and drain into colander. Halve the potatoes while still warm and toss with a small amount of the dressing to coat. Set aside to cool.

Heat a grill pan, if using, over high heat, then decrease the heat to medium-high. Coat the grill grids with oil or oil the grill pan. Brush the tuna steaks with olive oil and lightly season with salt and pepper on both sides. Grill uncovered, turning once, for about 4 minutes on each side for medium-rare. Remove from the heat and let rest for 3 minutes. Break into large pieces, about 3 inches or so.

Toss the lettuce in a large bowl with about 2 tablespoons of the dressing and salt and pepper to taste. In a small bowl, toss the tomatoes with 1 tablespoon of the dressing and salt lightly. Toss the beans with a small amount of salad dressing to coat just before serving.

Arrange the beans, potatoes, tuna, lettuce, tomatoes, olives, and egg wedges in sections on a platter. Sprinkle with the parsley and serve. Drizzle each serving with dressing and sprinkle capers on the tuna.

# Spanish-Style Potato Salad with Saffron-Aioli Dressing

Who doesn't love crispy, salty potatoes? This simple Spanish-influenced dish is a fine accompaniment to grilled fish. The saffron-scented aioli dressing is also wonderful tossed with pasta or on other seasonal vegetables. This dish is even more stunning when made with Peruvian purple potatoes.

SERVES 6 AS A SIDE DISH

8 unpeeled red potatoes

Olive oil, for brushing

2 tablespoons chopped fresh oregano leaves

2 tablespoons fresh thyme leaves

Coarse sea salt, for sprinkling

1 to 1$\frac{1}{2}$ cups Saffron-Aioli Dressing (recipe follows)

1 tablespoon chopped fresh flat-leaf parsley

1 tablespoon finely chopped green onion

Prepare a medium heat fire (375°F) in a wood-fired grill.

Slice the potatoes lengthwise into $\frac{1}{2}$-inch-thick slabs. Pat dry, then brush with olive oil. Sprinkle on both sides with the herbs and salt.

Oil the grill grids and cook the potato slices until golden and crisp, about 8 minutes on each side.

Transfer to a cutting board and sprinkle with sea salt. Stack the slabs and cut them into $\frac{1}{2}$-inch slices. Toss with the dressing while still warm. Garnish with the parsley and green onion.

## SAFFRON-AIOLI DRESSING

MAKES ABOUT 1$\frac{1}{2}$ CUPS

Small pinch (about 20 strands) of saffron threads

1$\frac{1}{2}$ tablespoons warm water

2 large egg yolks

1 large clove garlic, minced

$\frac{1}{4}$ teaspoon salt

$\frac{3}{4}$ cup extra-virgin olive oil

2 teaspoons freshly squeezed lemon juice

Freshly ground black pepper

Soak the saffron threads in the warm water in a small bowl for 20 minutes. Combine the egg yolks, garlic, and salt in a deep bowl and whisk to blend. You may also use a blender. Very gradually add the olive oil in a very thin stream, whisking constantly until about half of the oil has been added. Take care not to add the oil too quickly, or the aioli will separate. Add the saffron and its soaking water, then swirl the lemon juice around in the saffron-soaking bowl to catch any remaining saffron essence. Whisk the lemon juice into the aioli. Add a few grinds of pepper. Cover and refrigerate for at least 4 hours or up to 48 hours.

# CHAPTER 6

# Campfire Cooking

Nothing tastes better than food cooked on a campfire. **Camp food is simple food** cooked in an uncomplicated way, by baking, grilling, roasting, or smoking. Whether cooking at camp in a forest or at the beach, campfire cooking creates fond memories of great-tasting food.

The recipes in this chapter are for one-dish comfort foods cooked directly in or over the fire. Some are versions from my childhood campouts, others from times spent with friends. Campfire cooking can be done on the coals, in the coals, or above the coals on a grate, or over flames on sticks, skewers, or a spit. Equipment is minimal, and no fancy accessories are needed. Accordingly, instead of providing temperature ranges with these recipes, I've included information for judging a fire's heat with the hand-test method (see page 17 for a detailed guide). For the best results, use seasoned cast-iron or steel cookware. If it's cold outside and you yearn for some campfire cooking, use your indoor fireplace to cook great fireside food.

# Campfire Pork and Beans

Many camping menus include pork and beans. You can use ham, salt pork, bacon, or leftover pulled pork to season the beans. If using canned beans, rinse well and add for the last half hour of cooking. An excellent source for dried heirloom beans is Rancho Gordo (see Resources). Chipotle powder adds a little kick to this recipe.

**SERVES 8 TO 10 AS A SIDE DISH OR MAIN COURSE**

2 cups dried pinto or navy beans, rinsed, picked over, and soaked overnight

3 tablespoons canola oil

1 tablespoon cumin seeds

1/2 cup chopped onion

1 cup diced salt pork or bacon

6 juniper berries, bruised

1 teaspoon chipotle chile powder

4 cloves garlic, thinly sliced

1 teaspoon dried oregano

2 1/2 quarts water, or more as needed

2 tablespoons tomato paste

2 tablespoons brown sugar

1 teaspoon kosher salt

Prepare a medium-hot campfire (a 3-second fire) or a medium-hot fire (450°F) in a wood-fired grill.

Drain the beans and place in a Dutch oven or deep pot. Add water to cover by 3 inches. Place on the grate set over a campfire and cook on a low boil until just tender, about 1 hour, depending on the freshness of the beans. Cover for the last 30 minutes of cooking.

In a Dutch oven, heat the oil and add the cumin. Fry briefly until fragrant, then add the onion and salt pork. Cook until lightly browned, 5 to 10 minutes. Drain off any fat. Drain the beans then add tho the Dutch oven along with the juniper berries, chipotle powder, garlic, oregano, and enough water to cover. Bring to a simmer, cover, and cook for about 1 1/2 hours, until the meat and beans are tender. Stir in the tomato paste, brown sugar, and kosher salt. Uncover and cook to reduce the sauce slightly. Taste and adjust the seasoning.

# Smoked Chicken Stew with Herb Dumplings

My mother often cooked this dish when my family camped out. If you have leftover cooked chicken, use that instead of the smoked chicken, though the smoky taste is great in this dish.

SERVES 8 AS A MAIN COURSE

8 cups chicken stock

8 slices bacon, chopped

1 pound leeks (white part only), cut into 1/2-inch-thick
    slices and rinsed (see note on page 65)

3 stalks celery, cut into 1/2 inch slices

2 carrots, unpeeled and cut into 1/2-inch-thick slices

1 pound unpeeled red potatoes, cut into 1-inch pieces

1 celery root, peeled and coarsely grated or cut
    into 1/2-inch dice

12 ounces smoked chicken, shredded

1 teaspoon kosher salt

1 1/2 teaspoons dried tarragon

2 teaspoons fresh thyme leaves

1/3 cup minced fresh flat-leaf parsley

1 cup heavy cream

Pinch of freshly ground white pepper

DUMPLINGS

2 cups all-purpose flour

2 teaspoons baking powder

1 teaspoon kosher salt

2 tablespoons herbes de Provence

1/2 cup milk, at room temperature

1/3 cup butter, melted

2 large eggs, beaten

3 tablespoons grated Parmesan cheese

Prepare a campfire or wood-fired grill for cooking with indirect heat.

Bring the stock to a simmer in a large stockpot. Keep warm on the fire.

Brown the bacon in a Dutch oven until lightly crisp. Remove the bacon and one-third of the fat. Add the leeks and sauté for 5 minutes. Add the celery and carrots and sauté for 5 minutes. Add the potatoes, celery root, and warm stock and bring to a boil. Cook for 10 minutes, then add the smoked chicken, salt, tarragon, and thyme. Return to a simmer. Cover and cook at a low boil until the potatoes are tender, about 20 minutes. Stir in the parsley, bacon, and cream. Add the white pepper and additional salt to taste.

To make the dumplings, stir the flour and baking powder together in a bowl. Stir in the salt and herbs. Beat the milk, butter, and eggs together in a bowl. Stir into the dry ingredients until just combined. Stir in the cheese.

Place the dumplings by spoonfuls on the top of the stew, cover, and cook for 10 to 12 minutes, until the dumplings are plump but firm. Take the cover off for the last 5 minutes if a smokier flavor is desired from the fire.

Serve in bowls with one or two dumplings per serving.

# Over-the-Coals Bistecca Fiorentina

In this campfire version of an Italian classic, the steak is cooked on the coals, though *bistecca fiorentina* is traditionally cooked on a grill over the coals. Of course you can make it on a very hot grill or griddle pan if you choose, but it's fun to watch your steak cook directly on the coals. Choose the best steak you can afford. Add a side of creamy White Tuscan Beans with Sausage (page 119) and you've got a magnificent yet simple meal. *Buon appetito!*

**SERVES 4 AS A MAIN COURSE**

1 (2-pound) Porterhouse or T-bone steak, 2 inches thick

Kosher salt and freshly ground black pepper

1 teaspoon dried thyme

2½ cups arugula leaves

1 clove garlic, minced

2 tablespoons olive oil, plus more for drizzling (optional)

Juice of 1 lemon

Coarse sea salt or smoked or citrus salt for garnish
     (see page 187)

Shavings of Parmesan cheese

Prepare a hot fire in a campfire or wood-fired grill, then let the coals burn down to hot chunks of embers (a 6- to 7-second fire).

Place the steak directly on the hot coals and sear. Turn the steak and season generously with salt and pepper. Cook for 5 to 6 minutes, until the steak is charred on one side and can easily be removed from the coals. Turn and season with more salt, pepper, and the thyme. Cook for 5 to 6 minutes on the second side for medium-rare. If using a grill, the time needed for cooking will be 5 minutes more or so per side since the meat is above the coals rather than in the coals. Remove from the heat and let rest for 5 minutes.

Toss the arugula with the garlic, the 2 tablespoons olive oil, the lemon juice, and salt to taste.

Carve the steak into ¼-inch-thick diagonal slices. Serve immediately, topped with the arugula salad, coarse sea salt or smoked salt, and shavings of Parmesan cheese. Drizzle with more olive oil if desired.

# Salmon and Corn Chowder

This chowder is easy to make and requires only one pot! The salmon comes out tender and is a good match with the dill and potatoes. For a smokier flavor, roast the ears of corn directly over the fire before removing the kernels. If you don't have fresh salmon, frozen will work fine, or you can use smoked salmon. If using smoked salmon, cut back on the salt for seasoning.

SERVES 6 AS A MAIN COURSE

3 tablespoons olive oil

2 stalks celery, cut into 1/2-inch slices

8 ounces unpeeled small red potatoes, cut into 1-inch cubes

1 teaspoon kosher salt

1 1/4 teaspoons freshly ground white pepper

1 bunch green onions, coarsely chopped, including half
 of greens

1 1/2 cups corn kernels (about 2 ears)

4 cups fish or chicken stock

1 cup heavy cream

2 pounds salmon fillets, skin and pin bones removed,
 cut into 2-inch pieces

Grated zest and juice of 1 lemon

1/4 cup minced fresh dill

Prepare a campfire or wood-fired grill for cooking with indirect heat.

Heat the olive oil in a large, heavy saucepan or Dutch oven over medium heat and sauté the celery for 3 minutes. Add the potatoes, salt, and pepper and cook, stirring occasionally, for 5 minutes. Stir in the green onions and corn and add 2 cups of the stock. Bring to a boil, then reduce the heat, cover, and simmer until the potatoes are almost tender, about 15 minutes.

Add the cream and simmer, uncovered, until the potatoes are tender, 5 to 7 minutes. Stir in the salmon and lemon zest and simmer gently until the salmon is just cooked through, 3 to 4 minutes. Add more stock as needed and lemon juice to taste. Taste and adjust the seasoning.

Serve in bowls, topped with the dill.

# Split Pea Soup with Ham and Alder-Smoked Sea Salt

This recipe from author and cooking teacher Linda Carucci is a family favorite that she and I adapted for the wood-fired environment. The smokiness imparted is a great match with the ham. Use the ham bone to make a batch of this thick, satisfying soup to eat for supper during the week.

**SERVES 6 TO 8 AS A FIRST COURSE OR MAIN COURSE**

1 1- to 2-pound ham shank, cracked, or 1 ham bone

3 quarts chicken or vegetable stock or water (low-sodium, if using canned stock)

1 pound (about 3½ cups) dried green split peas, rinsed and picked over

2 large leeks (white and light green parts only), chopped and rinsed

1 large yellow onion, chopped

3 carrots, peeled and thinly sliced

1 stalk celery, sliced

6 sprigs thyme, or 1 teaspoon dried thyme

3 cloves garlic, crushed, or more to taste

1 bay leaf

1 teaspoon alder-smoked sea salt, plus more for seasoning (see note)

½ teaspoon freshly ground black pepper, plus more for seasoning

Prepare a hot fire (a 2-second fire) in a campfire, fire pit, or wood-fired oven.

Put the ham shank and stock in a 6-quart cast-iron or clay pot. Bring to a boil over high heat, then reduce the heat to a simmer. As the stock is heating, skim off any white foam that rises to the surface. Simmer until no more foam rises to the surface, about 10 minutes. Add the remaining ingredients and bring to a boil over high heat, stirring occasionally. Move to indirect heat at a lower temperature to simmer, cover, and cook until the vegetables and split peas are tender. Transfer the ham shank to a plate and set aside until cool enough to handle.

Pass the soup through a food mill into a clean 6-quart pot. Be sure to scrape the bottom of the food mill and add to the pot of soup. Alternatively, remove and discard the bay leaf and thyme sprigs and puree the soup in batches in a blender or food processor.

Trim off the skin and fat from the ham shank and cut the meat into ½-inch pieces. Add the meat to the soup.

If necessary, reheat the soup over medium heat in the oven. Taste and adjust the seasoning.

### ALDER-SMOKED SEA SALT

This smoky salt is fantastic in this soup. You can also use it in barbecue sauce, as it contributes a natural smoky flavor that's quite wonderful. The salt is smoked for twenty-four hours over red alder until it absorbs the wood's full, rich aroma (see page 187).

# Cheese and Prosciutto Panini with Smoky Romesco Sauce

Panini are pressed and griddled Italian sandwiches that can be filled with any number of simple fillings. They can be made with focaccia, soft rolls, or other breads. My favorite bread for this nutty, smoky combination is multigrain. Smoky Romesco Sauce flavors the bread and is also used for dipping.

SERVES 6 AS A LUNCH MAIN COURSE

2 tablespoons olive oil

6 cups spinach leaves

3 large cloves garlic, blanched (see page 192) and minced

Kosher salt

2 (1-pound) loaves artisan multigrain bread, cut into
　　½-inch-thick slices

6 tablespoons unsalted butter, at room temperature

½ cup Smoky Romesco Sauce (page 188)

14 ounces Gruyère cheese, thinly sliced

6 ounces sliced prosciutto, cut into lengthwise strips

Heat the olive oil in a skillet over medium-high heat and sauté the spinach until wilted. Stir in the garlic and a little salt. Set aside to cool slightly, then press in a sieve with the back of a large spoon to squeeze out moisture.

Spread the bread slices on one side with the butter and place, buttered side down, on a cutting board. Spread a thin layer of romesco sauce on each slice. Cover with slices of cheese, then prosciutto, and spread with wilted spinach. Top one side with a few more slices of cheese and close the sandwich.

Prepare a hot fire (a 2-second fire) in a campfire.

Preheat a cast-iron grill pan or skillet. Grill the sandwich over low heat until the bread is toasted on the bottom and the cheese is beginning to melt, about 7 minutes. Flip over and then press the sandwich flat by placing a heavy skillet on top of it. Grill until browned on the second side. Repeat with the remaining sandwiches.

Cut each sandwich in half and serve with the remaining romesco sauce alongside for dipping.

# Smoky Seafood Paella

In Spain, the native land of paella, this classic dish is often prepared over a live fire. Georgeanne Brennan and I adapted this recipe from *The Mediterranean Herb Cookbook* on a wood-fired grill at her home, using onions, garlic, peas, and fresh herbs from her garden. You can use fresh or frozen calamari. The quality of the ham and chorizo is very important, so shop for the recommended types. If you can't find them in your local store, shop online at The Spanish Table or La Tienda (see Resources). One of the secrets to this dish is that the herbs are added in layers. The second secret is to cook it over a wood fire!

SERVES 6 TO 8 AS A MAIN COURSE

1 pound cleaned calamari

1 teaspoon saffron threads

1 cup boiling water

2 teaspoons mixed dried thyme, rosemary, and sage

1/4 cup extra-virgin olive oil

2 yellow onions, chopped

4 cloves garlic, minced

2 large red bell peppers, seeded and cut into 1/4-inch-wide strips

3 1/2 cups Spanish short-grain or arborio rice

8 to 12 cups chicken broth

1/2 pound serrano ham or prosciutto

1 pound Spanish chorizo sausage, cut into 1-inch pieces

1 pound firm white fish fillets, cut into 1-inch pieces

4 large ripe tomatoes

2 cups green peas

1 1/2 pounds mussels, scrubbed

1 1/2 pounds clams, scrubbed

1 pound medium shrimp in the shell

1 teaspoon minced fresh thyme

1 teaspoon minced fresh oregano

Prepare a medium-hot fire (a 3-second fire) in a campfire or wood-fired grill.

Cut the calamari bodies into 1/2-inch-wide rings and set aside with the tentacles. In a small bowl, combine the saffron threads and boiling water and let stand until ready to use.

Place a 12-inch paella pan or other wide, shallow pan on a grate above the campfire or grill grate. Sprinkle in the dried herbs and stir for a few seconds to toast. Add the olive oil, onions, and garlic and cook, stirring, until the onions are translucent, about 3 minutes. Add the bell peppers and cook for another 3 minutes, or until they begin to soften. Add the rice and continue to cook, stirring, until the rice glistens and has changed color slightly. Add 6 cups of the broth and the saffron water and bring to a boil. Add the calamari, ham, chorizo, fish, and tomatoes and cook for 5 minutes. Add the green peas. Cook until most but not all of the liquid has been absorbed. From time to time, add more broth if it evaporates too quickly from the heat and the rice begins to stick. Continue stirring the rice and adding broth as needed until the rice is cooked.

Distribute the mussels, clams, and shrimp on top of the rice and push down slightly into the rice. Let them cook, without stirring, for about 10 minutes or until the shrimp are evenly pink and mussels and clams have opened. Remove the paella from the heat. Sprinkle with the fresh herbs, cover lightly with aluminum foil or a cloth and let stand for 5 minutes to allow the flavors to blend. Discard any mussels or clams that have failed to open. Serve hot.

# Garlicky Steamed Clams

This recipe is simple but packed with flavor. You can substitute other shellfish, such as mussels or shrimp or cracked crab, or a combination of all of these. This version gives a nod to Provence, using herbes de Provence and Pernod. The rich liquor created by the combination of the shellfish, garlic, wine, and herbs is the best part! Bake up some No-Knead Dutch Oven Bread (page 85) to accompany this delightful dish.

**SERVES 4 AS A FIRST COURSE OR MAIN COURSE**

2 tablespoons olive oil

4 to 6 large cloves garlic, sliced

2 cups dry white wine or vermouth

2 cups water or shellfish stock

2 bay leaves

1/2 teaspoon dried thyme, or 1/4 teaspoon herbes
    de Provence

Pinch of red pepper flakes (optional)

3 1/2 pounds small Manila clams, scrubbed

Fine sea salt or kosher salt

4 tablespoons unsalted butter

1/2 cup minced fresh flat-leaf parsley

3 tablespoons Pernod (optional)

Juice of 1 lemon

Prepare a hot fire (a 2-second fire) in a campfire or wood-fired grill.

Heat the olive oil in a Dutch oven or clay pot over direct heat. Move the pot to indirect heat, add the garlic, and sauté for 2 minutes. Add the wine, water, and bay leaves and move back to direct heat to bring to a low boil. Stir in the thyme and optional pepper flakes and place the clams in the liquid. Cover and move to indirect heat to cook until the clams open, about 10 minutes. Add salt to taste. Stir in the butter, parsley, and Pernod and cook, uncovered, for 10 minutes. Add lemon juice to taste and serve hot with crusty bread.

# Fire-Roasted Crab

The best way to serve this northern California specialty is on a table lined with newspapers. Here, boiled Dungeness crab is roasted in the shell in a cast-iron pan over a wood fire. It is equally wonderful roasted in a wood-fired oven. The deep, rich flavor of the roasted crab is extraordinary, especially when served with Wood Roasted Artichokes (page 105).

**SERVES 4 AS MAIN COURSE**

2 crabs (4 to 4½ pounds total) Dungeness crabs, cooked and cleaned

Olive oil, for drizzling

4 cloves garlic, thinly sliced

2 lemons, cut into 8 wedges

¼ cup dry white wine

⅛ teaspoon red pepper flakes (optional)

Sea salt

Prepare a medium heat fire (a 4- to 5-second fire) in a campfire or wood-fired grill, oven, or cooker.

Break apart the crab bodies and legs. Place them in a large cast-iron skillet or clay baker and drizzle with olive oil. Place slices of garlic under the crab and tuck wedges of lemon between the pieces of crab. Add the wine and cover lightly with aluminum foil. Roast over indirect heat for 10 minutes, then remove the foil and cook for another 10 minutes, or until the shells are toasted. Toss with the pepper flakes and salt to taste. Serve hot, with warm crusty bread.

### CRAB STOCK

Save the roasted crab shells and roast them further in the clay baker until well colored. Cover with water in a stockpot and simmer for 30 minutes, then let cool and strain. Cover and refrigerate for up to 3 days, or freeze for up to 3 months.

# Smoky Barbecued Oysters

What could be more fun than popping open oysters on the grill or on the coals of a fire? Large oysters work best for the grill. Or you can nestle them in a skillet lined with rock salt. In either case, the cooking skill needed to make mouth-watering oysters is minimal. The basic rule: Don't overcook the oysters! Here, they're served with an Indian-spiced barbecue sauce that's cooked over the fire for added flavor.

### SERVES 4 AS A FIRST COURSE

24 oysters in shell, scrubbed

SMOKY MASALA BARBECUE SAUCE

3 tablespoons olive oil

1 small onion, finely chopped

2 cloves garlic, minced

1/3 cup distilled white vinegar

1 1/2 cups tomato sauce

Liquid from the barbecued oysters

1/4 cup packed light brown sugar

1 teaspoon sweet pimentón (Spanish smoked paprika)

1/4 teaspoon garam masala

1/2 teaspoon cumin seeds, toasted and ground

Dash of Worcestershire sauce

Kosher salt and freshly ground pepper

Prepare a hot fire (a 2-second fire) in a campfire or wood-fired grill.

Place the oysters, deep-shell side down, on the campfire grate or grill over direct heat and cook until they open, 6 to 7 minutes. They may open only slightly. Leave them on the fire for another minute but no longer. There should still be juice in the shell when removed from the heat. Reserve the oyster liquid for use in the sauce.

To make the barbecue sauce, heat the oil in a medium skillet over medium heat and sauté the onion until tender, 5 minutes. Add the garlic and sauté for another 5 minutes. Add the vinegar and stir well. Stir in the tomato sauce and oyster liquid and bring to low boil. Stir in the brown sugar to dissolve. Add the pimentón, garam masala, cumin seeds, and Worcestershire sauce. Cook for 5 minutes, then remove from the heat and let cool. Add water if needed to thin. Add salt and pepper to taste. Use now, or cover and refrigerate for up to 1 week.

Using a heat-resistant glove, break off the top shell and serve in the deep shell. Place on a platter lined with rock salt and serve hot, with a dollop of barbecue sauce.

# No-Knead Dutch Oven Bread

This is a very simple bread to make either at the campsite or at home. It requires no kneading, and is baked in a Dutch oven or clay baker. This bread's flavor is developed through extended fermentation.

MAKES ONE 1$\frac{1}{2}$-POUND LOAF

2$\frac{1}{2}$ cups all-purpose flour, plus more for dusting

$\frac{1}{2}$ cup whole-wheat flour

$\frac{1}{4}$ teaspoon instant yeast

2 teaspoons kosher salt

1$\frac{3}{4}$ cups water, at room temperature (about 70°F)

Cornmeal (optional)

Coarse sea salt

In a large bowl, combine the flours, yeast, and salt. Stir in the water until blended. The dough will be rough looking and a bit sticky. Place in a covered container and let rest for 12 to 18 hours at room temperature. The dough is ready when bubbles appear on the surface.

Gently empty the dough out on a lightly floured board and dust the dough with flour; then, using a bowl or bench scraper, fold the dough over on itself two times. Cover with a kitchen towel and let rest for 15 minutes.

Line a bowl large enough to hold the risen dough with a flour sack or linen kitchen towel. Generously coat the bowl portion of the towel with all-purpose flour or a combination of flour and cornmeal.

Flour your hands and the work surface (if needed), gently shape the dough into a ball, and quickly place seam side down in the floured bowl. Cover the dough with the ends of the towel and set aside to rest for about 2 hours, or until doubled in size.

Prepare a hot fire (a 2-second fire) in a campfire or wood-fired oven, cooker, or grill. Heat an empty 4-quart baking pot (cast iron, ceramic, or clay) in the hot oven or on the grill 30 minutes before baking.

Remove the pot from the oven and, holding one hand under the towel, gently turn the dough out into the pot, seam side up. Any ragged edges are fine. They will become crispy and crunchy in the bake. Sprinkle with coarse sea salt.

If cooking over coals, place a sheet of aluminum foil over the ridge of a Dutch oven and put the lid in place. Put 10 or so hot coals over the top of the lid and return the oven to the fire or place the legs over hot coals. Bake for 20 minutes. Remove the lid and bake for another 15 minutes or more, until the loaf is a deep golden color. Slide out of the pot and let cool on a wire rack. Let rest for 1 hour before serving.

### VARIATIONS

You can use only all-purpose flour if you choose, or you can adjust the flour quantity to include ground nuts or flaxseed. Add some chopped herbs, fire-roasted garlic, or citrus zest to it just before folding the dough for even more layers of flavor.

# Mom's Crazy Chocolate Cake

When I was growing up, my Mom made this magical chocolate cake that doesn't use eggs and is mixed in the pan it's baked in. It's the most moist chocolate cake I've ever tasted, and because no refrigerated ingredients are used, it's perfect for camping. Crazy cake dates back to the Depression, but I don't know where my mother found this recipe; it's always been in her handwriting.

MAKES ONE 8-INCH-SQUARE CAKE

1½ cups all-purpose flour

5 tablespoons unsweetened cocoa powder

1 cup sugar

1 teaspoon baking soda

½ teaspoon kosher salt

1 teaspoon distilled white vinegar

1 teaspoon vanilla extract

5 tablespoons canola oil

1 cup water

FROSTING

1 cup confectioners' sugar

2 tablespoons unsweetened cocoa powder

2 tablespoons unsalted butter, at room temperature

½ teaspoon vanilla extract

1 tablespoon milk, or as needed

Prepare a medium heat fire (a 4-second fire) in a wood-fired oven or cooker, or prepare a campfire grill for cooking over indirect heat.

Sift the flour, cocoa powder, sugar, baking soda, and salt into a greased 8-inch-square cake pan. Make three wells in the dry ingredients. Pour the vinegar into one, the vanilla into another, and the oil into the third. Pour the water over all and stir until smooth. Level out the surface and cover with aluminum foil. Bake for 35 minutes, or until a toothpick inserted in the center comes out clean. Set aside to cool.

To make the frosting, stir the sugar and cocoa powder together in a bowl. Beat in the butter and vanilla until smooth. Stir in just enough milk to make the frosting soft and spreadable. Spread over the cake and let set for 30 minutes before cutting and serving.

# Dad's Favorite: Hobo Cake

My dad enjoyed few desserts. For him, they needed to be simple and not very sweet. This uncomplicated cake, which he dubbed hobo cake because making it at campfire represented the simple life of a hobo, was one of his favorites. We enjoyed it at the campfire as well as around the comfort of our fireplace. You don't have to be an accomplished baker to make this cake; it's very easy and quite tasty. You can top each serving with a dollop of crème fraîche to bring it into the present time.

**MAKES ONE 12-INCH CAST-IRON-SKILLET CAKE**

1 tablespoon unsalted butter

2½ cups all-purpose flour, plus more for dusting

1 cup granulated sugar

¾ cup packed brown sugar

1 teaspoon ground nutmeg

½ teaspoon kosher salt

¾ cup canola oil

2 teaspoons ground cinnamon

½ cup finely chopped walnuts

1 teaspoon baking soda

1 teaspoon baking powder

1 large egg, beaten

1 cup buttermilk

Prepare a medium heat fire (a 4-second fire) in a wood-fired oven or cooker, or prepare a campfire with a grate for cooking over indirect heat. Grease a cast-iron skillet with the butter, then dust with flour.

Combine the flour, sugars, nutmeg, salt, and oil in a bowl. Stir to blend. Transfer ½ cup of this mixture to a small bowl and stir in the cinnamon and walnuts. Set aside to use for the topping.

Add the baking soda and baking powder to the remaining flour mixture, then add the egg and buttermilk. Stir to blend. Pour into the prepared pan and sprinkle with the topping. Bake for 20 minutes, or until a toothpick or knife inserted into the center comes out clean.

# CHAPTER 7

# Wood-Fired Roasting

Whether with a spit, wood planks, herb-lined or salt-filled pans, in cast-iron skillets or in embers, wood-fire roasting has been practiced for hundreds of years in many cultures. The flavors created are unlike those of any other roasted foods. Wood-fired food is beautifully caramelized on the outside and flavored by the fire; the inside is moist and tender. Roasting takes place at a lower temperature range (325° to 450°F) than grilling or campfire cooking, but at higher temperatures than baking and slow cooking. It invariably yields extraordinarily tasty results.

Oven-roasting is usually done in a shallow baking dish. Roasting traditionally requires fat either in the food or added during the cooking process. Oven-roasting can be done on a grill or in a ceramic cooker where an enclosed cooking chamber (oven) can be created. In this situation, the heat circulates around the food being cooked.

Spit-roasting of meat or poultry has the heat source either under it or at the side of it, and the food is slowly rotated over the fire. Spit-roasting is self-basting and can be done in a fireplace or on a grill using a rotisserie.

Fire- or ember-roasting is done directly in the embers of a fire. It requires the food to be enclosed in a wrapping of aluminum foil in the case of meats and fish, or a natural skin or husk in the case of fruits or vegetables. The food is placed directly into the embers and turned frequently until cooked.

# Spit-Roasted Leg of Lamb with Tzatziki

This great-tasting dish from Joanne Weir takes you back to medieval times and spit-roasting at the hearth. You can also roast it over a grill or roast in an oven. This version is flavored with Greek herbs and served with a yogurt-cucumber sauce. Accompany with Pita Bread (page 44).

SERVES 8 AS A MAIN COURSE

1 (5- to 6-pound) leg of lamb, butterflied and trimmed

2 cloves garlic, thinly sliced, plus 1 clove minced

Salt and freshly ground black pepper

1/4 cup chopped fresh flat-leaf parsley

2 tablespoons chopped fresh chives

2 tablespoons chopped fresh mint

1/2 teaspoon chopped fresh rosemary

1/2 teaspoon chopped fresh thyme

1/2 teaspoon chopped fresh oregano

4 tablespoons extra-virgin olive oil

Tzatziki (recipe follows)

Prepare a very hot fire (500°F) in a fireplace or a medium-hot fire (425°F) in a wood-fired oven.

Lay the lamb flat on the work surface with the exterior of the leg on the work surface. With the point of a knife, make several incisions in the lamb and insert a slice of garlic into each incision. Season lightly with salt and pepper.

In a small bowl, stir together the parsley, chives, mint, rosemary, thyme, oregano, minced garlic, and 3 tablespoons of the olive oil.

Spread the herb mixture evenly over the exposed side of the lamb. Roll and wrap the lamb around the spit and secure with kitchen twine or small metal turkey skewers. Brush the outside of the lamb with the remaining 1 tablespoon olive oil and season with salt and pepper.

Place the spit 6 to 8 inches from the fire and spit-roast the lamb, using an electric or battery-powered unit to rotate the spit consistently, until an instant-read thermometer inserted into the thickest part of the lamb registers 135°F for medium-rare, about 1 hour. Alternatively, put the lamb in a roasting pan and roast in the oven for 1½ to 2 hours, or until an instant-read thermometer inserted into the thickest part of the lamb registers 135°F. Let the meat stand for at least 10 minutes before slicing. Serve with Tzatziki.

# TZATZIKI

MAKES 2¹/₄ CUPS

2 cups whole or nonfat Greek yogurt

¹/₄ teaspoon salt

¹/₂ English cucumber, peeled and seeded

3 to 4 cloves garlic, minced

2 tablespoons minced fresh mint

1¹/₂ tablespoons minced fresh dill

1 tablespoon extra-virgin olive oil

1 tablespoon freshly squeezed lemon juice

Combine the yogurt and salt in a bowl and stir to blend. Turn into a cheesecloth-lined sieve placed over a bowl and let drain for several hours to remove excess moisture in the yogurt.

Meanwhile, shred the cucumber to make 1 cup. Spread the shredded cucumber on paper towels and sprinkle lightly with salt. Let drain for 30 minutes. Using paper towels, squeeze out the excess moisture.

Combine the yogurt, grated cucumber, garlic, mint, dill, and olive oil in a bowl. Mix well. Add the lemon juice to taste. Taste and adjust the seasoning. Use now, or within 1 day.

# Mustard and Lemon Chicken

This tasty roasted chicken recipe is from Cheryl and Bill Jamison and is adapted from their book, *Smoke & Spice*. We made this together at their home in Santa Fe and adapted it to the Big Green Egg, which works perfectly at 250 to 275°F. The birds were a beautiful tobacco color from the oak lump charcoal smoke. If you like, add any leftover rub to the mop for additional flavor.

SERVES 6 TO 8 AS A MAIN COURSE

RUB

6 tablespoons Hungarian paprika

2 tablespoons freshly ground black pepper

2 tablespoons celery salt

2 tablespoons sugar

1 tablespoon garlic powder

1 tablespoon dry mustard

1 teaspoon cayenne pepper

Zest of 1 to 2 lemons, minced


2 tablespoons unsalted butter

1 tablespoon Worcestershire sauce

2 (3 1/2-pound) chickens

1 onion, cut into thin wedges

1 lemon, cut into thin wedges


LEMON MOP (OPTIONAL)

1 1/2 cups chicken stock

3/4 cup freshly squeezed lemon juice

1/2 onion, chopped

1/2 cup unsalted butter

1 tablespoon Worcestershire sauce

1 tablespoon yellow mustard

1/2 cup water

The night before you plan to barbecue, combine all the rub ingredients in a small bowl.

In a small saucepan, melt the butter and stir in the Worcestershire sauce. Remove the giblets and excess fat from the chickens. Massage the chickens thoroughly inside and out with the butter mixture, working the mixture as far as possible under the skin without tearing it. Reserve about one-third of the rub and spread the rest all over the chickens, again massaging inside and out and over and under the skin. Place the chickens in large self-sealing bags and refrigerate.

Prepare a low heat fire (200° to 220°F) in a wood-fired cooker.

Remove the chickens from the refrigerator. Rub them again with the dry rub and then insert the onion and lemon wedges into the body cavities. Let the chickens stand at room temperature for about 30 minutes.

To make the mop, mix together all the ingredients in a saucepan and heat over low heat.

Place the chickens in the smoker, breast down. Cook for 2 hours, basting with the mop every 30 minutes, or as needed. Turn the birds breast side up and cook for 1 1/2 hours longer, or until the legs move freely and an instant-read thermometer inserted in a thigh or breast registers 180° to 185°F.

Let the chickens stand for 5 to 10 minutes under a loose tent of aluminum foil. Remove the lemons and onions from the cavities, carve the chicken, and serve.

# Chicken Toscana Cooked Under Bricks

Roasting chicken under bricks creates an evenly golden skin and moist, succulent meat. The bricks keep the chicken weighted down and somewhat flattened, which allows it to cook evenly and more quickly than if roasted whole. Brining the chicken keeps the flesh moist. Any number of vegetables can be roasted as part of this dish, but I prefer just tomatoes and shallots.

SERVES 4 AS A MAIN COURSE

1 (3- to 3½-pound) chicken (preferably free-range)

BRINE
8 cups water
²/₃ cup salt
²/₃ cup sugar

4 cloves of garlic, thinly sliced lengthwise
2 sprigs thyme
2 sprigs rosemary
Kosher salt
½ teaspoon freshly cracked black pepper
¼ cup olive oil, plus more for rubbing
1½ pounds firm, ripe plum tomatoes, halved lengthwise
1 pound unpeeled shallots, halved lengthwise

Remove the giblets and any lumps of fat from the inside of the chicken. To brine the chicken, combine all the brine ingredients in a large nonreactive container and submerge the chicken completely. Refrigerate for at least 2 to 4 hours or overnight. Rinse and pat very dry inside and out, then let come to room temperature.

Prepare a hot fire (475° to 500°F) in a wood-fired oven. Push the embers off to the left rear of the oven and add a small log to maintain a low fire. The oven should be about 450°F when the chicken goes in. Double-wrap 4 bricks in aluminum foil.

Place the chicken, breast side down, on a work surface. With a pair of poultry shears, split the bird lengthwise along the backbone. Open it out and press down with the heel of your hand to crack the bone and flatten completely. Turn the chicken skin side up and, approaching from the edge, slide a finger under the skin of each of the breasts, making 2 little pockets. Create a pocket on the thickest area of each thigh. Shove herb sprigs and slivers of garlic into each pocket. Season the chicken liberally with salt and cracked pepper and rub with olive oil.

Using a sharp knife, make slits in the skin near the tail and tuck the wing tips in to secure. The bird should be as flat as possible to ensure even cooking.

Heat the olive oil over medium-high heat in a large cast-iron skillet until almost smoking. Place the chicken, skin side down, in the skillet. Weigh the chicken down with the foil-wrapped bricks. Place the skillet in the center of the wood-fired oven and roast until the skin is golden, about 15 minutes—you will hear the chicken sizzle. Remove the bricks and turn the chicken over. Replace the bricks, add the tomatoes and shallots, and return to the oven for 15 minutes or until the tomatoes and shallots are slightly blistered and the juices run clear when the thighs are pierced. Peel the shallots before serving.

Transfer the chicken to a platter and tent loosely with aluminum foil. Let rest for 10 to 20 minutes. Carve and serve warm or at room temperature, with the tomatoes and shallots and drizzled with the roasting juices.

# Roasted Beef Tenderloin with Root Vegetables and Horseradish Sauce

Beef tenderloin is very lean and cooks quickly. Cooking over wood enhances the flavor of the meat as well as the vegetables. You can substitute small potatoes if you can't find parsnips. This can easily be made in a conventional oven, though the smoky flavors will be missing. The Horseradish Sauce is a version my mom always made to serve with prime rib at Christmas.

SERVES 8 AS A MAIN COURSE

3 tablespoons oil

Kosher salt and freshly ground black pepper

1 (3-pound) beef tenderloin

3 slices bacon

3/4 cup beef stock

1/3 cup dry white wine

1 bay leaf

1 pound baby carrots, trimmed

6 to 8 pearl onions or shallots, peeled

2 parsnips, peeled and cut into 2-inch-long pieces

Minced fresh chives, for garnish

Prepare a hot fire (450°F) in a wood-fired oven or cooker.

Heat a Dutch oven or cast-iron skillet over medium-high heat, then add the olive oil to heat through. Lightly salt and pepper the tenderloin. Sear on all sides.

Cover the meat with the bacon strips and add the stock and wine to the pan. Add the bay leaf and vegetables to the liquid. Cover and roast for about 20 minutes, basting several times with the liquid. Uncover and roast for 5 to 10 minutes, or until the vegetables are tender and an instant-read thermometer inserted in the center of the meat registers 135°F. Remove the roast and vegetables from the pan and let rest on a cutting board for 10 minutes. Skim off the excess fat from the roasting liquid. Return the Dutch oven to medium heat and cook to reduce the liquid by one-third. Reserve the reduced juices for the horseradish sauce.

Slice the beef and serve with the vegetables and sauce. Garnish with the chives.

## HORSERADISH SAUCE

MAKES ABOUT 1 1/2 CUPS

2 tablespoons unsalted butter

Reduced cooking liquid from tenderloin (above)

4 tablespoons prepared horseradish sauce

1 cup crème fraîche or heavy cream

Pinch of cayenne pepper

Kosher salt

1 tablespoon minced fresh chives

Melt the butter in a small saucepan over medium-high heat. Stir in all of the reduced liquid and the prepared horseradish sauce. Remove from the heat and stir in the crème fraîche. Return to medium heat and cook to reduce slightly. Add the cayenne and salt to taste. Remove from the heat and stir in the chives. Serve warm.

# Roasted Chard-Wrapped Salmon

Many Mediterranean cuisines wrap fish in leaves for grilling or roasting. This version uses Swiss chard. You can use either the white-stemmed variety or one of the colorful rainbow chards. Use fresh grape or fig leaves for an even more flavorful result.

SERVES 8 AS A MAIN COURSE

8 (4-ounce) salmon fillets, skin and pin bones removed

Olive oil, for rubbing and brushing

1½ tablespoons sweet pimentón (Spanish smoked paprika)

1½ tablespoons ground fennel seeds

½ teaspoon kosher salt, plus more for sprinkling

Pinch of freshly ground white pepper

8 to 10 Swiss chard leaves, stalks removed

Roasted Corn and Smoky Tomato Salsa (page 188)

Prepare a medium-hot fire (400°F) in a wood-fired oven or cooker, or prepare a medium-hot fire in a wood-fired grill prepared for cooking with indirect heat.

Rub the salmon with olive oil. Combine the pimentón, fennel powder, the ½ teaspoon salt, and the pepper in a small bowl. Spread the dry mixture out on a baking sheet. Roll the salmon pieces in the mixture to coat, then set aside.

In a large sauté pan, bring 1½ inches of salted water to a boil and blanch the chard leaves until they are just wilted and pliable. Remove from the pan and immediately transfer to a bowl of ice water for about 2 minutes. Transfer to paper towels to drain. Lightly salt on one side.

Lay a salmon fillet on each chard leaf about one-third of the way in from the end nearest you. Fold in the sides of the leaves, then the top and bottom to cover the fish (use extra leaves for each packet if necessary). Set aside. Brush each packet with olive oil and place folded side down on a baking sheet. Bake for 15 to 20 minutes, or until the chard is crisp and the salmon barely opaque throughout. Remove from the oven and let rest for 5 minutes. Serve the packets topped with the salsa.

# Salt-Roasted Whole Fish

Salt-roasting is a traditional Mediterranean technique for cooking fish. The salt crust creates an almost impenetrable barrier that traps the moisture and allows the natural juices of the fish to remain—the salt never penetrates into the food itself. Salt-roasting is a great hybrid of steaming and roasting, and can be used to cook meat, poultry, and vegetables.

SERVES 6 AS A MAIN COURSE

3 pounds (one box) plus 3 cups kosher salt

6 large egg whites, lightly beaten until foamy

2 teaspoons fennel seeds

1 (4-pound) whole sea bass, arctic char, tuna, or salmon,
    cleaned and scaled

1/2 teaspoon white peppercorns

3 cloves garlic, thinly sliced

3 sprigs rosemary or thyme or fennel fronds

1 orange, zested in strips and flesh cut into thin slices, plus
    more orange slices for garnish

1 tablespoon olive oil

Green olive tapenade (page 192)

Prepare a medium-hot fire (425°F) in a wood-fired oven or cooker.

In a large bowl, mix 3 pounds of the salt and the egg whites together into a thick paste. Stir in the fennel seeds.

Rinse the fish and pat dry. Measure and set aside 1 teaspoon of salt. Using the remaining salt, line a rimmed baking sheet with ½ inch of salt.

Season the cavity of the fish with the 1 teaspoon salt and the peppercorns. Insert the garlic, herb sprigs, orange zest, and slices of orange into the cavity. Rub the fish with olive oil and place on the salt-lined baking sheet.

Pat the salt paste over the fish to cover it about ½ inch thick. The tail does not need to be covered. Make sure the coating is even.

Roast for 25 to 35 minutes, or until the crust is hard and golden. The timing depends on your oven, the type and size of fish you're using, and the temperature of the fish when it went into the oven. If you're not sure if the fish is done, break some of the salt away and check to see if the flesh pulls away from the bone. If it doesn't, leave it in the oven for a few more minutes.

Remove the fish from the oven and let rest for about 15 minutes. Serve at the table. Gently crack the salt crust away from the fish with a meat pounder or the handle of your chef's knife. Have a bowl handy for the scraps of salt crust. Portion and serve the fish garnished with orange slices, with the tapenade alongside.

# Tea-Brined Mahogany Duck

Smoking duck with tea is an Asian tradition. This recipe uses a fragrant brew of Darjeeling tea, fresh ginger, and star anise for roasting rather than smoking. The tea brine gives the duck a dark, smoky flavor. My favorite way of roasting the duck is in the La Caja China box roaster. The duck comes out a beautiful mahogany color and is succulent and moist, with a smoky taste and a crisp skin. An Asian-influenced basting sauce is used as a mop a few times over the course of roasting. Tea brine can be made with other black teas, such as oolong or Earl Grey. It can also be used for roasted chicken or even pork.

SERVES 4 TO 6 AS A MAIN COURSE

TEA BRINE

8 cups water

1/2 cup Darjeeling or oolong tea leaves

3 slices fresh ginger

2 star anise pods

1/3 cup soy sauce

1/4 cup honey

2 (3-pound) ducks, or 1 (5-pound) roasting chicken

BASTING SAUCE

1 cup reserved tea brine (above)

1 tablespoon hoisin sauce

4 tablespoons soy sauce

3 tablespoons honey

To make the brine, combine the water, tea leaves, ginger, and star anise in a saucepan and bring to a boil. Remove from the heat and let steep for 30 minutes. In a large nonreactive container, combine the steeped tea, soy sauce, and honey and stir until the honey is dissolved. Refrigerate for 1 hour.

Add the bird(s) to the brine; refrigerate ducks for 4 hours, chicken for 6 hours. Keep the bird(s) submerged by placing a plate on top to weight down and at a temperature of not more than 40°F. Remove from the brine 1 hour before cooking. Rinse and pat dry.

Prepare a medium-hot fire (400°F) in a wood-fired oven or cooker.

To make the basting sauce, combine all the ingredients in a bowl and stir until the honey is dissolved.

continued

To roast in a box roaster, place the bird(s) breast side down on a wire roasting rack in a roasting pan or clay baker and baste with the basting sauce. Light the charwood once the bird(s) is in place. Roast, covered, with indirect heat for 1 hour. Being careful not to pierce the skin, turn over, baste, and roast for 30 to 45 minutes, or until an instant-read thermometer inserted in a thigh registers 175° to 180°F.

To roast in a wood-fired oven or ceramic cooker such as a Big Green Egg, place the bird(s) breast side down in a roasting pan and baste with the basting sauce. Roast for 1 hour. Being careful not to pierce the skin, turn over, baste, and roast for 30 to 45 minutes, or until an instant-read thermometer inserted in a thigh registers 175° to 180°F.

Let sit for 10 minutes before carving and serving.

# Mushroom-Rubbed Plank-Roasted Steak

Plank cooking is a great technique for other foods besides fish. Steak cooked on a plank stays moist because of the damp smoke created by the soaked wood. The plank keeps the meat from drying out, and it also helps prevent flare-ups when grilling. In this recipe, the plank lends subtle smoky tones that harmonize with the roasted-mushroom rub. A garnish of smoked sea salt complements the earthy flavors.

Aromatic wood planks for cooking can be purchased today at many kitchenware stores. More choices are available online (see Resources). Alder, cedar, hickory, maple, and oak are best for cooking. (See wood chart, page 11.)

SERVES 4 AS A MAIN COURSE

$\frac{1}{2}$ teaspoon kosher salt

$\frac{1}{4}$ teaspoon freshly ground pepper

6 tablespoons roasted mushroom powder

4 (8-ounce) beef tenderloin steaks, $1\frac{1}{2}$ inches thick

Smoked or flavored sea salt (page 187), for garnish

Crumbled blue cheese, for garnish

Soak four 1-inch-thick roasting planks (7 inches by $11\frac{3}{4}$ inches) in water for 1 hour. Prepare a medium heat fire (375°F) in a wood-fired cooker for both direct and indirect cooking. The grate where the plank will be placed should be about 8 inches above the heat source.

Combine the salt, pepper, and mushroom powder in a small bowl. Pat the steaks dry and rub all over with the dry mixture.

Drain the planks and mark on one side by placing over direct heat either on a grate or over coals until lightly charred. Turn the planks over and rub them very lightly with olive oil, and move to indirect heat.

Heat a cast-iron skillet over high heat. Sear the steaks on both sides, then transfer to the charred side of the planks. Cover the cooker so that smoke surrounds the food and imparts flavor. Roast for 12 to 15 minutes for medium-rare. Remove steaks, planks and all, from the heat and let rest for 5 minutes before serving. The steaks can be served on the planks or on plates. Garnish with smoked salt and a dollop of crumbled blue cheese.

# Wood-Roasted Antipasti Platter

This is not your basic antipasti. Serving a beautiful platter of wood-roasted seasonal vegetables, cured meats, hand-crafted cheeses, home-cured olives, and smoke-kissed crusty bread to family and friends as a prelude to dinner is an artful way to honor guests. This is just what chef Chris Bianco does at his restaurant, Pizzeria Bianco, in Phoenix, Arizona. Chris's wood-fired pizzas are now legendary, but his wood-roasted antipasti platter *sings*. I hope you will enjoy my version, and create many versions of your own.

### SERVES 6 AS A FIRST COURSE

1 pound meaty mushrooms (porcini, chanterelles, maitake, portobellos)

Olive oil

Sea salt

1 pound each of 3 to 4 assorted vegetables, such as beets, baby carrots, parsnips, red bell peppers, eggplant, spring onions, radicchio, asparagus, and/or Brussels sprouts

1 head garlic

6 shallots

3 to 4 sprigs rosemary, thyme, or marjoram

1 handful of quality brine- or oil-cured olives, mixed or single variety

Serving wedges of one hard aged cheese, such as manchego or pecorino

Slices of one stellar cured meat, such as salami or prosciutto

Prepare a medium heat fire (350° to 375°F) in a wood-fired oven or cooker, or cool down a previously fired oven to 250°F for slow-roasting overnight.

Slice the mushrooms lengthwise, toss in olive oil and salt, and place in a small roasting pan. Cut other vegetables into bite-sized pieces or, if baby vegetables, leave them whole. Toss each type of vegetable in olive oil and salt and place each vegetable in its own small roasting pan. Roast the vegetables in the oven until caramelized and tender.

Roast red peppers whole directly on the floor or in the embers of the oven until well blistered, about 10 minutes. Place in a bowl, cover, and let stand for 15 minutes, then peel, seed, and cut into strips.

Roast the head of garlic until soft. Cut the shallots in half lengthwise, toss with olive oil, salt, and the sprigs of herbs. Roast in the oven until golden, caramelized, and tender. Warm the olives and the cheese in the wood-fired oven just before serving.

Platter up and serve with crusty bread, fresh olive oil, and your favorite wine. *Buon appetito!*

# Mushroom-Artichoke Ragout

This delicious stew of roasted baby artichokes, trumpet mushrooms, and asparagus is a nod to spring. Deborah Madison and I developed this recipe at her Santa Fe home using ingredients from the local farmers' market and topped it with a lovely goat cheese from northern New Mexico. Upon returning home to Northern California, I roasted the ragout in a clay baker in my wood-fired oven, which further highlighted the earthy flavors. It's easy to prepare, and the rich broth and meaty mushrooms are so satisfying. All you need is a few hunks of crusty bread and some beautiful cheese and you have a robust supper.

SERVES 4 AS A FIRST COURSE

8 baby artichokes or large artichoke hearts

1 pound asparagus, trimmed and peeled

1 pound fresh meaty mushrooms, such as porcini

4 cloves garlic, sliced

Strips of lemon zest

Salt and freshly ground black pepper

Olive oil, for drizzling

2 long sprigs thyme

1 bay leaf

1½ cups dry white wine

Juice of ½ lemon

Prepare a medium heat fire (350° to 375°F) in a wood-fired oven or cooker. Preheat a clay baker at the edge of the hearth.

Peel the outer leaves from the baby artichokes until reaching the light green leaves. Trim the stem and cut away any parts of the heart that were in contact with the outer leaves. Cut artichokes in half lengthwise and remove any thistle choke. Cut the artichoke hearts into ¼-inch-thick slices. Cut the asparagus on the diagonal into 2-inch-long pieces. Clean and trim the mushrooms, then cut lengthwise into ¼-inch-thick slices. Toss all of the vegetables in a bowl along with the garlic, lemon zest, and some salt and pepper, then drizzle with olive oil.

Layer the mixture in the heated clay baker and add the thyme and bay leaf. Cover with the white wine and place on the floor of the oven. Roast until the vegetables are tender and the mushrooms are golden, about 30 minutes. Remove from the heat and stir in the lemon juice. Taste and adjust the seasoning.

# Wood-Roasted Artichokes

As soon as it's artichoke season, I often make this dish when I'm firing the oven for making bread or pizza. It's so very simple in both ingredients and technique, you'll want to make it often. After you've baked your bread, throw this dish in the oven for a quick accompaniment to your meal. The heat from the oven slightly caramelizes the outer leaves of the artichokes and the skins of the lemons. You'll be amazed at how flavorful and sweet artichokes taste cooked this way! The lemons and juices are used to make a dipping sauce.

SERVES 4 AS A SIDE DISH

2 artichokes

Fine sea salt

Olive oil, for braising

2 lemons, cut into wedges or 1/4-inch rounds

Prepare a hot fire (450°F) in a wood-fired oven, or let the oven cool down from a hotter bread bake. Push the pile of embers to the left rear of the oven.

Remove a few of the outer leaves from the artichokes. Cut the artichokes in half and remove the chokes. Lightly salt the exposed surface with sea salt. Place the artichokes, cut side down, in a cast-iron skillet. Fill the skillet with 1/2 inch or so of olive oil and add water to bring the liquid level to about 1 inch. Add the lemon pieces in between the artichokes. Place the skillet in the oven about 5 inches from the embers. Roast for 12 to 15 minutes, or until tender. Remove from the oven and place the skillet on a wire rack to cool slightly.

TIP

Use the juices from the roasting to make a simple aioli to serve with the artichokes, or make a simple dipping vinaigrette by whisking olive oil into the juices.

# Best-Ever Brussels Sprouts

Brussels sprouts are misunderstood. They are often served overcooked, mushy, with not a lot of flavor. When wood-fire roasted along with shallots, however, they become caramelized, subtly smoky, and sweet.

SERVES 4 AS A SIDE DISH

1 pound Brussels sprouts

3 large shallots, cut into 1/2-inch wedges

1/4 cup olive oil

Kosher salt

1 1/2 tablespoons Dijon mustard

1/2 cup dry white wine

1/2 teaspoon freshly ground white pepper

1/4 teaspoon dried savory (optional)

Prepare a medium-hot fire (400° to 425°F) in a wood-fired oven or cooker.

Cut the Brussels sprouts in half lengthwise. Toss, along with the shallots, in the olive oil with salt to taste.

Choose a medium cast-iron skillet or clay baker that will snugly fit the Brussels sprouts and shallots in a single layer; oil the pan or baker. Place the Brussels sprouts and shallots, cut side down, in the pan and place, uncovered, in the oven or cooker to roast. If using a wood-fired oven, the pan can sit directly on the hearth.

Make a sauce by combining the remaining ingredients. After 10 minutes, pour the sauce over the vegetables. Cover lightly with aluminum foil or a lid and return to the cooker. Continue to cook for another 10 minutes, or until the Brussels sprouts are very soft. Uncover and roast for a few more minutes, or until browned.

# Salt-Roasted Potatoes

These potatoes are the best roasted potatoes you've ever tasted! The radiant heat from the salt crisps the skin while holding in the natural moisture of the potatoes. This method can be used for roasting other vegetables, such as beets, sweet potatoes, and even small acorn squash. The salt can be saved and reused for roasting another batch of vegetables. Or you can place some of the salt in a jar to add to the flavored-salt collection in your pantry.

SERVES 6 AS A SIDE DISH

5 pounds kosher or coarse sea salt

2 pounds small unpeeled red or Yukon Gold potatoes

2 sprigs rosemary

1 bay leaf

Prepare a hot fire (500°F) in a wood-fired oven or cooker.

Line a 6-quart Dutch oven, deep cast-iron spyder, or clay casserole with 1 inch of salt. Bury the potatoes in the salt and poke the rosemary and bay leaf into the salt. Pour the remaining salt over the potatoes to cover. Cover the pot and roast for 1 hour, or until the potatoes are tender. For a smokier flavor, leave the lid off the pot while roasting, but make sure the potatoes are well covered by at least 1 inch of salt.

Transfer the contents of the pot to a bowl and fish out the potatoes. Brush off any salt left on the potatoes. Serve whole, or smash with a fork.

# Roasted Tomatoes Provençal

In the south of France, beautiful large ripe tomatoes are often stuffed with herbs and bread crumbs, then served with grilled fish. Here, the tomatoes are wood-roasted for added flavor. You can play with other herbs such as dill or marjoram in the stuffing.

SERVES 8 AS A SIDE DISH

8 large, firm tomatoes

Kosher salt

1½ cups coarse fresh bread crumbs

6 tablespoons chopped fresh flat-leaf parsley

2 tablespoons fresh thyme leaves, plus thyme sprigs
    for garnish

¼ cup grated Parmesan cheese

4 cloves garlic, blanched (page 192) and minced

2 tablespoons capers, drained and rinsed

Freshly ground black pepper

¼ cup olive oil

Prepare a medium-hot fire (400° to 425°F) in a wood-fired oven or grill.

Cut the tops off the tomatoes and discard. Using a teaspoon or your finger, carefully seed the tomatoes, leaving the shells intact. Lightly salt the interior of the tomatoes. Place the tomatoes, cut side down, on paper towels to drain for 15 minutes.

Combine the bread crumbs, parsley, the 2 tablespoons thyme, the cheese, minced garlic, and capers in a small bowl. Add salt and pepper to taste.

Heat the olive oil over medium heat in a terra-cotta dish or skillet large enough to hold all the tomatoes.

Place the tomatoes, cut side down, in the dish or skillet and roast for 5 minutes. Remove from the heat and turn the tomatoes cut side up. Spoon 2 to 3 tablespoons of the bread-crumb mixture into each tomato and mound it on the top.

Spray the topping with cooking spray and lightly salt. Bake for 30 minutes or until the topping is browned. Garnish with thyme and serve.

## CHAPTER 8

# Clay-Pot and Cast-Iron Oven Cooking

One of the oldest methods of wood-fired cooking is in vessels of clay, glass, or metal. Today, clay and cast iron are the materials of choice because the cookware is extremely efficient, versatile, and well-suited to wood-fired cooking. As an additional benefit, the food cooked in clay or cast iron just tastes better. These cooking vessels, when well seasoned from use, absorb flavors from the food they cook. They also impart flavors back, along with adding valuable trace minerals to food being cooked. Over time, an exchange between the food and the pot develops, and the flavor of the food increases. For example, beans cooked in a clay pot, especially a seasoned one, over coals or in a wood-fired oven, will taste better than beans cooked any other way. And the more they're used, the better iron and clay pots get.

Here is Paula Wolfert on this phenomenon. From her book *The Slow Mediterranean Kitchen*: "When I try to explain why food tastes better when cooked in clay or seasoned iron, I fall back on the word *coddling*. These pots, in effect, coddle the food as if wrapping it in a warm blanket, then slowly bring out unctuous tenderness and a particular taste and aroma that food writers like to call *gout de terroir* (taste of the earth)."

As with wood-fired roasting, clay-pot and cast-iron cooking can be done in an oven, on a grill, or in a ceramic cooker. Both covered (moist-heat cooking) and uncovered (dry-heat cooking) methods are featured in this chapter.

# Tiella of Lamb with Fennel, Pecorino, and Potatoes

Paula Wolfert and I revised this fabulous dish of hers for cooking in my wood-fired oven. The key is to cook it until the lamb is falling-apart tender. The recipe is adapted from Paula's book, *The Slow Mediterranean Kitchen*. It comes from the southern Italian region of Apulia, where it is baked in a shallow terra-cotta dish called a *tiella*. You can make it entirely in the wood-fired oven, or cook the onions and brown the lamb on the stove top, then move it all to the oven to finish cooking.

### SERVES 4 TO 6 AS A MAIN COURSE

2 pounds lean boneless shoulder of lamb, cut into
    2-inch chunks

2 cups whole milk

2 bay leaves

1/4 teaspoon fennel seeds

1 sprig rosemary

2 cloves garlic, sliced, plus 1 clove whole

5 tablespoons olive oil

1 red onion, sliced

Salt and freshly ground pepper

Flour for dusting

2 1/2 pounds boiling potatoes, such as Red Bliss or
    Yellow Finn

1/2 cup chopped fresh flat-leaf parsley

3/4 cup grated aged sheep's milk cheese, such as
    pecorino sardo or pecorino toscano

1 cup fresh bread crumbs

Combine the lamb, milk, bay leaves, fennel, rosemary, and garlic in a large pot. Cover and let stand in a cool place for 4 to 6 hours.

Prepare a medium-hot fire (425°F) in a wood-fired oven or cooker.

Heat 2 tablespoons of the olive oil in a baking dish over medium heat and sauté the onion until pale golden, 10 to 15 minutes. Remove the lamb from the milk bath and pat the chunks dry with paper toweling. Reserve the milk and aromatics. Lightly salt and pepper the lamb, then dust with a little flour. Add the lamb to the same pan over medium heat and brown on all sides, about 10 minutes.

Meanwhile, peel the potatoes and cut into 1/8-inch-thick crosswise slices. Soak the potatoes in the reserved milk. Season the browned lamb with a little more salt and pepper. Transfer the onion and lamb to a side dish. Tilt the pan and remove any oil. Add a few tablespoons of water to the pan and stir to scrape up the browned bits from the bottom of the pan. Reserve the liquid.

Rub an ovenproof 2 1/2-quart clay baker with the clove of garlic, then lightly oil. Scatter the onion slices in the baker. Drain the potatoes, reserving the milk. Layer one half of the drained potatoes on top of the onions and sprinkle with pepper. Spread the meat in one layer; sprinkle with all of the parsley, half of the cheese, and half of the bread crumbs. Layer the remaining drained potatoes on top. Add the reserved pan liquid to the milk mixture and pour over the potatoes. Press down on the potatoes so there will be some room for expansion. Place the pan over low heat and slowly bring to a boil, about 15 minutes.

Sprinkle the top of the potatoes with the remaining cheese and bread crumbs and the remaining 3 tablespoons olive oil. Loosely cover with aluminum foil and set the pan on the floor of the oven to bake for about 15 minutes. Move to a cooler section of the oven (where it is about 325°F) and continue baking for 1 1/4 hours. Remove the foil and cook for another 30 minutes, or until crusty and golden. Let rest for 30 minutes, then serve warm.

# Soufflé Casserole of Chard, Goat Cheese, and Fresh Herbs

Often people are intimidated by the thought of making a soufflé, but soufflés are actually quite easy to make and are delicious. This simple version has seasonal herbs and greens and is baked as a casserole in a shallow dish. It doesn't have to be served before it deflates, because the amount of pouf is less important in this presentation. This casserole is wonderful for brunch or a light lunch served with some lightly dressed tender salad greens. If you want a traditional presentation, this same recipe can be made in an 8-cup soufflé dish.

SERVES 8 AS A SIDE DISH

2 cups grated Parmesan cheese

1 small bunch chard leaves

2 tablespoons olive oil

1/4 cup sliced shallots

1 cup chopped arugula leaves

1 tablespoon fresh marjoram leaves

1 tablespoon fresh mint leaves, torn into small pieces

Kosher salt and finely ground white pepper

BÉCHAMEL SAUCE

1 1/2 cups low-fat milk

1 large bay leaf

1 shallot, sliced

3 tablespoons unsalted butter

3 green onions (white part only), thinly sliced

3 tablespoons all-purpose flour

1/2 teaspoon Dijon mustard

Kosher salt and freshly ground white pepper

4 large egg yolks, beaten

1 cup crumbled fresh goat cheese

6 large egg whites

1/4 cup minced fresh flat-leaf parsley

Prepare a medium heat fire (375°F) in a wood-fired oven or cooker.

Butter an 8-cup gratin dish and dust with the Parmesan. Cut out the chard stems, dice them, and set aside. Chop the chard leaves; you should have about 2 cups.

Heat the olive oil in a cast-iron skillet over medium heat and sauté the diced chard stems and shallots until soft, 5 to 7 minutes. Add the chard leaves, arugula, herbs, and salt and pepper to taste. Sauté to wilt the greens, about 5 minutes. Remove from the heat and set aside.

To make the béchamel sauce, combine the milk, bay leaf, and shallot in a saucepan over medium heat. Bring to a low boil, then remove from the heat and let steep for 15 minutes. Discard the bay leaf and shallots. Set aside.

Melt the butter in a saucepan over medium heat. Add the green onions and sauté for 1 minute. Add the flour and stir for 3 minutes. Stir in the Dijon mustard. Gradually stir in the steeped milk until the sauce is thickened. Season with salt and pepper. Remove from the heat and set aside.

Stir the egg yolks into the béchamel sauce. Add the wilted greens and salt and pepper to taste. Add 3/4 cup of the goat cheese. In a large bowl, beat the egg whites until stiff, glossy peaks form. Fold half of the egg whites into the béchamel mixture, then the remaining half. Spoon the soufflé mixture into the prepared dish.

Top with the remaining goat cheese and the parsley. Place in the oven on a grate and bake for 25 to 30 minutes, until firm to the touch and golden. Serve hot.

# Crab Gratin with Potatoes, Leeks, and Spinach

Scalloped potatoes was one of my favorite childhood dishes. I've added the classic combination of crab and spinach to this version and lightened the sauce a bit by using milk instead of cream. You can substitute shrimp or lobster meat for the crab.

SERVES 8 AS A MAIN COURSE

1/4 cup olive oil

3 small leeks (white part only), sliced crosswise and rinsed

8 ounces fresh or frozen crabmeat, rinsed and drained

2 teaspoons Dijon mustard

1/4 teaspoon chili powder

1/8 teaspoon white Worcestershire sauce

1 (10-ounce) package frozen chopped spinach, thawed and drained

2 teaspoons chopped fresh tarragon

1/2 teaspoon kosher salt

Pinch of freshly ground white pepper

MORNAY SAUCE

3 tablespoons unsalted butter

3 tablespoons flour

2 cups milk

1 teaspoon freshly grated nutmeg

1 teaspoon grated lemon zest

1/2 teaspoon salt

1/8 teaspoon freshly ground white pepper

1 cup shredded Gruyère cheese

2 tablespoons dry sherry

1/2 cup toasted bread crumbs

3/4 cup shredded Gruyère cheese

2 pounds unpeeled red or Yukon Gold potatoes, very thinly sliced

Kosher salt and freshly ground white pepper

Prepare a medium heat fire (375°F) in a wood-fired oven or cooker.

Heat half of the olive oil in a small skillet over medium heat and sauté the leeks until wilted, about 7 minutes. Blend together with the crabmeat, mustard, chili powder, and Worcestershire sauce in a bowl and set aside. Heat the remaining olive oil in a saucepan over medium heat and sauté the spinach until most of the moisture has evaporated. Stir in the tarragon, salt, and white pepper. Remove from the heat, stir in the crab mixture, and set aside.

To make the Mornay sauce, melt the butter in a skillet over medium heat. When it has stopped foaming, stir in the flour and cook, stirring, for 3 minutes. Whisk in the milk, nutmeg, zest, salt, and pepper. Add the Gruyère and sherry. Cook, stirring, until thickened. Remove from the heat and set over a pot of simmering water.

In a small bowl, combine the bread crumbs and 1/2 cup of the Gruyère. Coat an 8-cup clay casserole or gratin dish with olive oil. Dust the bottom of the dish with the bread-crumb mixture. Line the dish with one-third of the potatoes, overlapping the slices lengthwise.

Blend one-third of the Mornay sauce into crab mixture. Lightly salt and pepper the potatoes in the gratin dish and cover with half of the crab mixture. Add another one-third of the potatoes, then cover with the remaining crab mixture. Layer with the remaining potatoes and then the remaining Mornay sauce. Bake for 25 to 30 minutes. Top with 1/4 cup Gruyère and bake for 10 minutes, or until the potatoes are tender and the cheese is browned. Remove from the oven and let stand for 10 minutes before serving.

# Three-Cheese Baked Penne with Pancetta

This is a grown-up mac and cheese with lots of rich Italian flair. Using three flavorful Italian cheeses and incorporating pancetta makes this hearty dish the ultimate comfort food. You can use a different shape of dried pasta as long as it has a cavity to hold the creamy sauce. Try other cheeses, too.

SERVES 6 AS A MAIN COURSE

3/4 cup plus 2 tablespoons grated pecorino romano cheese

2 1/2 cups heavy cream

Grated zest of 1 lemon

3/4 cup shredded Italian fontina cheese

1/4 cup ricotta cheese

Puree from 1 head roasted garlic (page 192)

1 teaspoon kosher salt

1/2 teaspoon red pepper flakes

1/4 cup olive oil

4 ounces pancetta, chopped

1 cup fresh bread crumbs

2 tablespoons fresh thyme leaves

1 pound penne rigate pasta

4 tablespoons chopped fresh flat-leaf parsley, for garnish

Prepare a medium heat fire (400°F) in a wood-fired oven or cooker.

Generously butter an 8-cup casserole and dust it with the 2 tablespoons pecorino romano.

Combine the cream, lemon zest, remaining 3/4 cup pecorino romano, the fontina and ricotta cheeses, pureed garlic, salt, and red pepper flakes in a large bowl. Heat the olive oil in a small skillet over medium heat and sauté the pancetta until crisp. Using a slotted spoon, transfer to paper towels to drain, reserving the fat. Coarsely crumble the pancetta.

Combine the bread crumbs and thyme in a small bowl and moisten with the reserved cooking fat from the pancetta. Lightly salt.

In a large pot of salted boiling water, cook the pasta for 10 minutes. Drain and add to the cream mixture. Toss in the crumbled pancetta (or leave to sprinkle over the bread-crumb topping, if you choose).

Fill the prepared dish with the pasta mixture and sprinkle on the bread-crumb mixture. Bake in the conventional oven or on a grate in the wood-fired oven until the pasta is bubbly, golden brown, and a bit crisp on the edges, 15 to 20 minutes. Serve hot, garnished with parsley.

# Eggplant, Red Pepper, and Goat Cheese Gratin

This recipe is adapted from a recipe my friend Deborah Madison shared in her book, *Vegetarian Suppers from Deborah Madison's Kitchen.* It is absolutely gorgeous! Purple eggplant, red peppers, and golden saffron custard are a beautiful combination. Eggplant and red peppers are the perfect ingredients to cook in a wood-fired oven, as they both take on the wonderful smokiness of the fire. In this recipe, the eggplant is lightly sautéed in a skillet in the oven. The red peppers, tomatoes, and garlic are roasted whole, directly on the floor of the oven or in the embers, until the skins are blistered and beautifully charred. When cooled, they are skinned and seeded. Peppers roasted this way have a more complex flavor than when blackened on the stove top.

## SERVES 6 TO 8 AS A MAIN COURSE

1½ pounds small globe eggplants, cut into
    ⅓-inch-thick slices

3 tablespoons olive oil

Salt, for sprinkling, plus ½ teaspoon

2 red bell peppers

3 medium tomatoes

1 head garlic

2 tablespoons fresh thyme leaves

½ teaspoon herbes de Provence (optional)

Pinch of sugar

Pinch of freshly ground black pepper

1 cup toasted bread crumbs

3 tablespoons almond meal

12 ounces fresh goat cheese, thinly sliced

⅓ cup oil-cured olives, pitted and halved

½ cup fresh whole flat-leaf parsley leaves

2 large eggs

1½ cups Greek goat's milk yogurt

2 small pinches saffron threads, soaked in a few
    tablespoons hot water

Prepare a medium heat fire (400°F) in a wood-fired oven or cooker.

Sauté the eggplants in the olive oil in a skillet over medium heat on the stove top, or directly in the wood-fired oven or on the cooker. Cook for 2 minutes on each side, or until soft. Set the eggplant aside on paper towels to drain. Lightly salt both sides.

When there are some hot embers in the fire, place the red peppers, tomatoes, and garlic on the floor of the oven or bottom of the cooker near the embers. Rotate them frequently as the skins blister and char. Cook until the skins are fully charred, 5 to 7 minutes for the tomatoes and 10 minutes for the peppers. Cook the garlic until the skin is slightly charred and the cloves are soft, about 5 to 7 minutes.

In a small bowl, squeeze the roasted garlic cloves out of their skins and mash with a fork to form a paste. Place the charred tomatoes and peppers in a bowl, cover with plastic wrap, and let sweat for 10 minutes. Remove the skins from the tomatoes and peppers. Slice open the peppers, remove the stems and seeds, cut into pieces about the same size as the eggplant, and set aside. Slice open the tomatoes and remove the seeds with your index finger or by squeezing gently. Dice the tomatoes and combine with the mashed garlic, herbs, sugar, ½ teaspoon salt, and pepper.

Brush a clay casserole with olive oil and dust with a mixture of the bread crumbs and almond meal. Reserve the rest of the bread-crumb mixture. Line the casserole with one-third of the tomato mixture, then layer on slices of eggplant, goat cheese, red pepper, and bread-crumb mixture, followed by half of the olives. Salt and pepper each layer. Repeat the layers, finishing with the tomato mixture, parsley, and goat cheese. Whisk the eggs with the yogurt and ½ teaspoon salt. Stir in the saffron liquid and pour the custard over the entire casserole.

Bake for 25 minutes in a wood-fired oven, or until the casserole is bubbly and golden on top. Remove from the heat and let stand for 10 minutes before cutting into portions and serving.

# Moroccan Tajine of Halibut, Potatoes, and Artichokes

This recipe from Georgeanne Brennan shows a classic way to cook in a tajine, layering flavors and food together for the slow, moist cooking. It includes the Moroccan sauce *sharmula*, which gives a spicy flavor and adds moisture to the fish during the cooking. You can make many variations on this dish, substituting chicken for fish or tomatoes and eggplant for artichokes.

SERVES 4 AS A MAIN COURSE

SAUCE

1 1/2 cup fresh cilantro leaves

1/2 cup fresh flat-leaf parsley leaves

4 cloves garlic

1/2 onion, chopped

1/4 cup extra-virgin olive oil

2 tablespoons freshly squeezed lemon juice

1 teaspoon freshly ground black pepper

1 teaspoon paprika

1/2 teaspoon ground cumin

1/4 teaspoon ground cinnamon

1 teaspoon salt


4 (5-ounce) halibut, sea bass, true cod, or other firm
　　fish steaks, each cut 1/2 to 3/4 inch thick

8 baby artichokes

2 tablespoons freshly squeezed lemon juice

2 teaspoons extra-virgin olive oil

2 unpeeled potatoes, very thinly sliced

Salt and freshly ground black pepper

16 oil-cured black olives

1/2 cup canned Italian plum tomatoes, chopped and juice
　　reserved, or 2 ripe red tomatoes, thinly sliced

1/4 cup chopped fresh cilantro leaves

1/4 cup chopped fresh flat-leaf parsley leaves

Prepare a medium heat fire (350°F) in a wood-fired oven or cooker.

To make the sauce, combine all of the ingredients in a blender and blend to a paste. Add a little more olive oil if needed. Alternatively, finely chop the cilantro, parsley, onion, and garlic, then mix with the remaining sauce ingredients.

Using half of the sauce, coat both sides of the fish. Cover and refrigerate for at least 1 hour or up to 3 hours. This will allow the flavors to blend.

Trim the artichoke stems and discard. Break off the outer leaves until you reach leaves that are pale yellow at the base. Cut off the upper one-third of the leaves. Trim the rough edges at the base. Cut the artichokes lengthwise into quarters. Add the lemon juice to a bowl of water and add the artichokes.

Add the olive oil to the bottom of the tajine, then add the potatoes. Sprinkle the potatoes with a little salt and pepper. Top the potatoes with a layer of fish. Scatter the artichokes and olives over and around the fish. Top with the remaining sauce, and finally with about 1/2 cup of the chopped tomatoes and their juices. Add a sprinkling of salt and pepper. To finish, top with the cilantro, parsley, and a little more salt and pepper.

Cover and bake until the potatoes are fork-tender, about 1 hour and 15 minutes.

To serve, bring the tajine to the table and lift the lid. Use a serving spoon or spatula to serve each person a piece of fish, some artichokes, olives, and potatoes.

# Baked Risotto with Asparagus and Swiss Chard

Risotto is typically made on the stove top with a fair amount of stirring to release the starch from the grains of rice. It can also be baked in a casserole, though it will be less creamy because less starch is released. Cooking it in a wood-fired oven adds a smoky flavor. The asparagus and Swiss chard are perfect additions in spring. You can use any of your favorite seasonal greens in their place. Diced butternut squash or yellow beets are terrific here too, as are the traditional mushrooms.

SERVES 6 AS A SIDE DISH

2 tablespoons olive oil

1 onion, finely chopped

Pinch of kosher salt, plus 1½ teaspoons

1½ cups arborio rice

2½ cups vegetable or chicken stock

½ cup dry white wine

1 large bunch chard leaves, chopped, stems cut out
        and reserved (about 4 cups)

1 pound thin asparagus spears, trimmed and cut into
        2-inch diagonal slices

¼ teaspoon freshly grated nutmeg

1½ cups grated Parmesan cheese

Prepare a medium heat fire (375°F) in a wood-fired oven or cooker.

Heat the olive oil over medium heat in a 6-quart Dutch oven or casserole dish. Add the onion and a pinch of salt and sauté until the onion is translucent, about 3 minutes. Add the rice, stirring to coat with the oil. Stir in the stock, wine, chard leaves and stems, asparagus, nutmeg, and 1½ teaspoons salt. Place in the oven, uncovered, and bring to a simmer. Cook for 5 minutes, then stir in half of the cheese and smooth the top. Sprinkle with the rest of the cheese and cover tightly with aluminum foil.

Place the baking dish back on the floor of the oven near the center. Bake until the rice is cooked through and has absorbed most of the liquid, about 20 minutes. The rice should be moist but not soupy. Remove the foil for the last 10 minutes of baking to create a beautiful golden crust and to add smoky flavor.

Serve immediately.

# White Tuscan Beans with Sausage

Luscious cannellini beans are one of my favorites, whether plain, drizzled with olive oil, or baked with melting garlic and rosemary. They can be cooked in a wood-fired oven, in embers in the fireplace, or over indirect heat on a grill. Cook the sausage at the same time. This recipe is extraordinarily easy to make, letting the clay pot and the fire be the star flavor contributors, along with the sausage.

**SERVES 6 AS A MAIN COURSE**

3 cups dried cannellini beans, rinsed, picked over, and
    soaked overnight

1/2 pound Italian sausage of choice

1 teaspoon kosher salt

6 cloves garlic, thinly sliced

1 (3-inch) sprig rosemary

1/4 cup extra-virgin olive oil, plus more for drizzling

2 cups balsamic vinegar (optional)

Prepare a medium-hot fire (350°F) in a wood-fired oven or grill prepared for cooking with indirect heat.

Drain the soaked beans and put them in a large clay bean pot. Add enough water to cover the beans by 2 inches. Cover and place in the oven or over indirect heat on a grill and bring to a boil.

Cut the sausage in half lengthwise and place cut side down in a clay baker. Roast in the oven until the fat is rendered; drain. Or, cook the sausage over direct heat on the grill. Cut the cooked sausage into bite-sized chunks or crumble. Set aside.

Add the salt to the beans and move to a cooler area of the oven or grill to gently simmer until the beans begin to soften, about 1 hour. Add more water if you can see the beans above the reduced liquid. Add the garlic, rosemary, and the 1/4 cup olive oil. Cover and continue to cook, stirring a few times, until the beans are tender and the garlic is soft. Add more water if all of the liquid has evaporated. The beans should be slightly saucy. Remove the rosemary and transfer 1 cup of the beans to a food processor to puree until smooth. Stir the pureed beans into the whole beans. Add the sausage and continue to cook until very tender.

Meanwhile, bring the balsamic to a simmer in a nonreactive saucepan over medium heat. Cook until reduced by about two-thirds, 20 to 25 minutes.

Remove the beans from the heat and generously drizzle with olive oil. Serve warm, drizzled with the reduced balsamic, if you like.

# Bouillabaisse

The traditional seafood stew of Provence is typically made with tomatoes, shellfish, local fish, and herbs, but this version is made without tomatoes, allowing the fish and saffron to be prominent. Cooking it over a wood fire adds a bit of smoke to the beautiful fish. Serve with a crusty baguette to soak up the flavorful broth.

SERVES 8 AS A MAIN COURSE

4 cups water

6 cups fish stock

12 ounces (16 to 20) shrimp in the shell

3 tablespoons olive oil

1 yellow onion, chopped

3 stalks celery, coarsely chopped

3 carrots, peeled and coarsely chopped

4 cloves garlic, minced

1/2 cup dry white wine or vermouth

1 teaspoon kosher salt

1/2 teaspoon fresh ground white pepper

1/2 teaspoon saffron threads

1 teaspoon fresh thyme leaves

2 bay leaves

2 1/2 pounds halibut, cod, or tilapia fillets, cut into
    1 1/2-inch pieces

4 ounces scallops, drained of liquid

1 dozen mussels, scrubbed

2 tablespoons chopped fresh flat-leaf parsley

Prepare a medium-hot fire (350°F) in a wood-fired oven, cooker, or grill.

Combine the water and stock in a stockpot and bring to a simmer over coals or on the floor of a wood-fired oven. Shell the shrimp and put the shells in the stockpot. Set aside and keep warm.

Heat the olive oil in a Dutch oven over medium-high heat on a grate over a grill or on the floor of a wood-fired oven. Add the onion, celery, and carrots and sauté for 5 minutes. Add the garlic and sauté for 2 minutes. Remove the shells from the warm broth and add three-quarters of the liquid to the sautéed vegetables. Add the wine, salt, pepper, saffron, thyme, and bay leaves; bring to a boil. Move to a cooler area of the oven and simmer for 15 minutes; discard the bay leaves. Return to a boil, add the fish, and simmer for 5 minutes. Add the remaining stock, the scallops, and mussels and cook for 2 minutes. Add the shrimp and cook for another 3 minutes. Taste and adjust the seasoning. Bring to a low boil for 1 minute.

Discard any unopened mussels. Stir in the parsley and serve in bowls.

# Two-Bean Pozole with Cumin Crème Fraîche

I love the Southwest of the United States and the foods of that region. This recipe features three ingredients borrowed from its Native American culture: corn, beans, and peppers. Here, the stew is made with vegetable stock, but you can also use chicken stock. Wood-roasted pork shoulder or chicken can be shredded and added to the dish for an even heartier meal. The heirloom beans come from my friend Steve Sando's company, Rancho Gordo. You can substitute other dried beans, but the flavor will be best if you use Rancho Gordo beans (see Resources). The stew can be made a day ahead and reheated just before serving. Any leftovers are terrific as a filling for tamales or enchiladas.

### SERVES 8 AS A MAIN COURSE

2 red bell peppers

2 poblano chiles

6 cups vegetable stock

3 tablespoons olive oil

2 onions, diced

4 carrots, peeled and diced

2 stalks celery, diced

Kosher salt and freshly ground pepper

2½ cups cooked Yellow Indian heirloom beans, drained

2½ cups cooked Ojo de Cabra heirloom beans, drained

3 cups cooked white hominy (canned or freshly made white pozole)

2 ancho chiles

6 cloves roasted garlic (page 192)

1 (14½-ounce) can crushed tomatoes, preferably fire-roasted

3 tablespoons fresh thyme leaves

1 tablespoon chopped fresh sage

2 tablespoons chopped fresh oregano, or 2 teaspoons dried Mexican oregano

1 cup dry sherry

Fresh cilantro leaves, for garnish

Cumin Crème Fraîche (recipe follows)

Prepare a medium heat fire (375°F) in a wood-fired oven or cooker.

When there are some hot embers in the fire, place the bell peppers and poblano chiles on the floor of the oven or grate of the cooker near the embers. Rotate them frequently as the skins blister and char. Cook until the skins are fully charred, 5 to 7 minutes for the poblanos and 10 minutes for the peppers.

Place the poblanos and peppers in a bowl, cover with plastic wrap, and let sweat for 10 minutes. Remove the skins from the poblanos and peppers, then slice open and remove the stems and seeds.

Bring the vegetable stock to a simmer in a pot on the stove top or in the oven or cooker.

Heat the olive oil in a 6-quart Dutch oven over high heat until just smoking. Add the onions, carrots, and celery and sauté until the onions are translucent, about 3 minutes. Add the bell peppers, poblanos, and salt and pepper to taste and sauté for 1 minute. Add the drained beans and hominy to the pot. Pour in 4 cups of the stock. Cover and transfer to the oven.

Heat a small cast-iron skillet over high heat on the stovetop or in the oven or cooker. Place the ancho chiles in the hot, dry pan and toast on both sides until fragrant and their color has darkened slightly, about 5 minutes. Remove from the pan and let cool, then slice open and remove the stems and seeds.

In a small bowl, squeeze the roasted garlic cloves out of their skins and mash with a fork to form a paste. Set aside.

After 30 minutes, stir the tomatoes, ancho chiles, roasted garlic, thyme, sage, and oregano into the pot with the beans. Add the sherry and more stock if needed to keep the beans covered. Cover and continue cooking for 40 minutes, checking the liquid level after 20 minutes and adding stock as needed. Uncover, add stock if needed, and cook for 15 minutes. Taste and adjust the seasoning. Remove from the oven and let stand for 10 minutes before serving.

Serve in bowls topped with cilantro and Cumin Crème Fraîche.

## CUMIN CRÈME FRAÎCHE

### MAKES 1 CUP

8 ounces crème fraîche
1 tablespoon cumin seeds, toasted and ground
Grated zest and juice of 1 lime
Kosher salt

Combine the crème fraîche, cumin, zest, and juice in a bowl and stir to blend. Add salt to taste.

# Smoky French Onion Soup

French onion soup topped with nutty Gruyère cheese is one of the best comfort foods ever! When cooked over a live fire, the deep, rich smoky flavors and aromas are intoxicating. Sweet onion varieties such as Vidalia, Maui, or red Bermuda make the best soup. Of course, if only basic yellow onions are available, by all means use those. A pinch of sugar added during the cooking of yellow onions will bring out their natural sweetness.

SERVES 8 AS A MAIN COURSE

2 tablespoons olive oil

3 tablespoons unsalted butter

5 pounds onions, thinly sliced

10 cups rich chicken or beef stock

1/2 cup Madeira wine

2 tablespoons Worcestershire sauce

1/2 teaspoon freshly grated nutmeg

2 large sprigs thyme

1 bay leaf

Kosher salt and freshly ground white pepper

2 cups shredded Gruyère cheese

8 slices baguette, toasted

Prepare a wood-fired oven or cooker for cooking with indirect heat.

Heat the olive oil over medium heat in a 4-quart Dutch oven or clay pot, then add the butter to melt. Add the onions and cook over indirect heat, stirring frequently, until they soften and just begin to brown, about 40 minutes.

Add 1/2 cup of the stock and move the pot to high heat. Stir to scrape up the browned bits from the bottom of the pot and cook until the stock has completely evaporated. Add the Madeira, Worcestershire sauce, and another 1/2 cup of the stock. Add the nutmeg and stir. Repeat, adding 1/2 cup stock and cooking until evaporated, 2 more times.

Add the remaining 8 cups of stock, the thyme, bay leaf, and salt and pepper to taste. Simmer for 20 minutes. Taste and adjust the seasoning. Remove the thyme sprigs and bay leaf.

Bring the oven to 400°F. Ladle the soup into deep heat-resistant bowls or crocks. Sprinkle half of the cheese over the soup and place a slice of the toast on top. Sprinkle the toast with the remaining cheese. Place the bowls on a baking sheet and bake until the soup bubbles and the cheese is melted and golden, 10 to 15 minutes. Serve hot.

# Curried Lentil and Vegetable Cassoulet

Cassoulet is a traditional French dish of white beans and various meats, cooked slowly for the flavors to blend. This fragrant vegetarian version uses Indian spices and lentils rather than white beans. It's wonderful as a main course or as a side dish with roasted chicken or fish.

**SERVES 8 AS A SIDE DISH, 4 AS A MAIN COURSE**

4 tablespoons olive oil

1 cup diced carrots

1/2 cup finely diced celery

6 to 8 cauliflower florets, halved

4 shallots, peeled and quartered

Kosher salt

2 cloves garlic, thinly sliced lengthwise

2 teaspoons grated fresh ginger

1¼ cups dried brown lentils

1 bay leaf

2 teaspoons cumin seeds, toasted

1 cup dry white wine

2½ cups vegetable stock

1 teaspoon ground turmeric

2 teaspoons garam masala

1/4 teaspoon cayenne pepper

2 to 3 tablespoons extra-virgin olive oil

Prepare a medium heat fire (375°F) in a wood-fired oven or cooker.

Toss 2 tablespoons of the olive oil, the carrots, celery, cauliflower, and shallots in a bowl. Spread on a rimmed baking sheet and lightly salt. Roast until soft and lightly caramelized, 20 to 25 minutes. Remove from the oven and set aside. Transfer any juices from the baking sheet to a small bowl and reserve.

Heat the remaining olive oil in a Dutch oven or clay casserole over medium heat and sauté the garlic and ginger for 5 minutes. Add the lentils, bay leaf, cumin, wine, reserved vegetable juices, and 1 cup of the stock. Cook for 5 minutes, then add the turmeric, garam masala, and cayenne and stir to blend. Cook until the stock is almost all absorbed, then add another cup. Repeat until the lentils are tender, 10 to 15 minutes (you may not need all of the stock). Add salt to taste and the extra-virgin olive oil and simmer for 1 minute more. Stir in the roasted vegetables and cook for another 10 minutes, then remove from the heat. Remove the bay leaf. Serve in shallow soup bowls.

# Fava Bean, Potato, and Escarole Soup

This soup has a wonderful bright, fresh flavor from the greens and lots of herbs. My favorite way of cooking this soup is in a pot made of micaceous clay (see sidebar opposite). The clay adds flavor and the added earthiness of the favas makes it heavenly! This version is pureed, though you can leave it chunky if you wish. You can substitute fresh peas for the favas and fresh spinach for the escarole. Make sure you use a really flavorful extra-virgin olive oil for finishing.

SERVES 8 AS A MAIN COURSE

1/4 cup olive oil

3 to 4 medium leeks (white part only), finely chopped
    (2 cups) and rinsed (see note page 65)

1 pound unpeeled red or yellow potatoes, cut into
    1/2-inch dice

Kosher salt

8 cups vegetable or chicken stock

6 cloves blanched garlic (page 192)

1 pound young escarole leaves, large stems removed

2 pounds fava beans, steamed, shelled, and skinned
    (see note page 65)

15 large fresh mint leaves

20 fresh basil leaves

Leaves from 1/2 bunch fresh flat-leaf parsley

1/4 cup fresh chervil or tarragon leaves (optional)

Freshly ground white pepper

1 tablespoon freshly squeezed lemon juice

1/4 cup Tuscan extra-virgin olive oil

1/2 cup crème fraîche, for drizzling

Roasted Garlic Croutons (recipe follows)

Prepare a medium heat fire (375°F) in a wood-fired oven or cooker.

Heat the olive oil in a clay pot or Dutch oven over medium heat. Add the leeks and cook until translucent, about 5 minutes. Stir in the potatoes. Cook for 2 minutes, then season with salt and add stock to cover. Add the garlic and simmer for 10 minutes. Add the escarole and 1/2 cup stock, cover, and simmer for 5 minutes. Add 1 cup of the fava beans and cook for 5 minutes.

Remove from the heat and add half of each of the herbs. Puree in a food processor or using an immersion blender. Add salt and pepper to taste. Refrigerate for 30 minutes or set aside to cool slightly. Add the remaining herbs and puree again. Stir in the lemon juice, then the extra-virgin olive oil. Taste and adjust the seasoning.

Serve at room temperature in shallow soup bowls for the optimum flavor. Drizzle each serving with crème fraîche and top with the remaining fava beans and a few croutons.

## ROASTED GARLIC CROUTONS

MAKES 3 TO 4 CUPS

1 demi baguette or small rustic bread such as pugliese,
    cut or torn into small cubes
3 cloves roasted garlic (page 192), mashed
1/3 cup olive oil
Kosher salt

Toss the bread, garlic, and olive oil together in a bowl. Add salt to taste. Spread on a parchment-lined sheet pan and toast in a preheated 375°F oven. Remove from the oven and set aside in a bowl to be used as garnish.

## Micaceous Clay Pots

Felipe Ortega is a Native American artist, potter, and shaman who has revived the art of crafting traditional pots of micaceous clay. The mica-filled clay is found in certain parts of New Mexico, and it is only that clay that is used to make these pots. Food cooked in them is unsurpassed in flavor (see Resources). For more on micaceous pottery, read *All That Glitters*, by Duane Anderson.

Pieces created by (clockwise from front left): Felipe Ortega, Priscilla Hoback, and La Chamba Colombiana.

# CHAPTER 9

# Baked on the Hearth: Savory Tarts and Galettes

One of my favorite subjects for my cooking classes is savory tarts and galettes. These can be free-form in style, with a wide range of crusts and fillings that can be combined with very flavorful results. Some have traditional pie dough crusts, while others have shells made with sliced potatoes, cornmeal, cooked rice, or leftover risotto. Some leftovers make great fillings as well. All can be baked on the hearth, my favorite way of preparing them.

These single-crust pies are baked on the floor of a wood-fired oven or on a pizza stone in a wood-fired cooker or on a grill. This baking process is similar to baking in a conventional oven, though it yields tarts with golden, crisp crusts and a slightly smoky flavor that often enhances the herbs and spices used. The recipes are easy to make, and the doughs are rustic and forgiving. If you don't have a wood-fired oven, you can create an indirect oven-like environment in a grill by placing a pizza stone on the grill grate and covering the grill.

# Shiitake and Roasted Garlic Tart

This is a simple yet elegant tart from Fran Gage. The roasted garlic custard makes a wonderful savory flan on its own, and the crust is perfect for other savory tarts (the recipe makes enough dough for 2 tarts; freeze the extra dough to use later). For even more complex flavor, roast the mushrooms as well as the garlic in the wood-fired oven.

MAKES ONE 9-INCH TART; SERVES 6 AS A MAIN COURSE

SAVORY TART DOUGH

1³/₄ cups unbleached all-purpose flour

¹/₂ teaspoon fine sea salt

13 tablespoons (1¹/₂ sticks plus 1 tablespoon) cold unsalted butter, cut into small pieces

6 tablespoons cold water

FILLING

3 unpeeled cloves garlic

2 tablespoons olive oil, plus more for drizzling

8 ounces shiitake mushrooms, stemmed and finely chopped

Fine sea salt and freshly ground black pepper

3 large eggs

1¹/₄ cups half-and-half

Prepare a medium-hot fire (450°F) in a wood-fired oven or cooker.

To make the dough, stir the flour and salt together in a bowl. Using your fingertips or a pastry blender, rub or cut the butter into the flour until some of the butter is in flakes and other pieces are the size of peas.

Stir in the water, 1 tablespoon at a time, until all of the ingredients are moistened. Form the dough into a ball. It will still look a little rough, with some streaks of butter. On a floured board, cut the dough in half, flatten each piece into a disk, and wrap in plastic wrap. Refrigerate for at least 1 hour or up to 3 days. The dough can also be frozen for 1 month.

Roll out 1 disk into an 11-inch round. The dough should be ¹/₈ inch thick. Transfer it to a 9-inch tart pan with a removable bottom and fit it into the pan. Run a rolling pin over the top to remove the excess dough. Refrigerate the lined pan while making the filling.

To make the filling, cut the stem ends from the garlic cloves, put the cloves in a small baking dish, and drizzle with olive oil. Roast until soft, about 20 minutes.

Meanwhile, heat the 2 tablespoons olive oil in a large skillet until it shimmers. Add the mushrooms and sprinkle with salt and pepper. Cook, stirring frequently, until the mushrooms soften, glisten, and squeak, about 5 minutes. Remove from the heat and let cool.

Remove the garlic from the oven and let cool for 10 minutes. Squeeze the insides of the cloves onto a work surface and chop finely. Place in a bowl. Whisk in the eggs and half-and-half. Sprinkle with salt and pepper.

Strew the mushrooms over the bottom of the lined tart pan and pour the custard over them. Put the pan on a parchment-lined baking sheet. Slide the sheet onto the hearth of the oven and bake for 35 to 40 minutes, until the crust is brown and the custard is puffed and golden brown. Let cool on a wire rack. Serve warm or at room temperature.

# Crispy Potato, Artichoke, Leek, and Gruyère Tart

Tart crusts can be made from other ingredients, including cooked spaghetti, polenta, and rice, or in this case, thinly sliced potatoes. The goal is to make a crisp, shallow vessel that will contain the filling without leaking. This is especially important when a custard filling is used. The baby artichokes in this recipe can be replaced by thinly sliced artichoke hearts.

MAKES ONE 10-INCH TART; SERVES 8 AS A MAIN COURSE

4 leeks (white part only), halved lengthwise

¼ cup olive oil

1 pound baby artichokes

2 tablespoons freshly squeezed lemon juice

½ cup dry white wine

2 teaspoons fresh thyme leaves

Kosher salt and freshly ground white pepper

1 pound red potatoes, very thinly sliced

2 large eggs

1½ cups ricotta cheese

½ cup milk

½ teaspoon cayenne pepper

2 teaspoons grated lemon zest

2 teaspoons minced fresh chives

2 cups shredded Gruyère cheese

¼ cup pine nuts, toasted (page 184)

Prepare a medium-hot fire (425°F) in a wood-fired oven or cooker.

Cut the leeks crosswise into half rings and rinse well. Heat 3 tablespoons of the olive oil in a terra-cotta baker, in the oven or cooker, and cook the leeks until translucent, about 7 minutes. Transfer to a bowl and set aside.

Remove the outer artichoke leaves, then thinly slice the artichokes lengthwise. Add the lemon juice to a bowl of ice water and place the artichoke slices in the water. Drain and pat dry the artichokes dry with paper towels. In the same clay baker, sauté the sliced artichokes in the olive oil left over from the leeks over medium-high heat in the oven or cooker until lightly browned, about 5 minutes. Add the wine and stir to scrape up the browned bits from the bottom of the pan. Add the thyme and salt and pepper to taste and cook for 3 minutes, or until the moisture is removed. Remove from the heat and set aside.

Toss the potato slices in the remaining olive oil in a bowl and lightly salt. Reserve 5 slices for the top of the tart.

Heat a 10-inch slope-sided skillet or clay baker on the stove top over medium-high heat and brush with olive oil. Remove from the heat and line the vessel with slices of potatoes, overlapping the slices to cover the bottom and sides of the pan. Lightly pepper. Place in the oven or cooker and bake until golden, about 15 minutes. Remove from the oven.

Combine the eggs and ricotta in a bowl and beat until blended. Add the milk, cayenne, lemon zest, chives, and salt to taste. Fill the potato crust with half of the Gruyère, then the leeks. Top with the artichokes, add the ricotta mixture, and top with the remaining Gruyère and a sprinkling of pine nuts.

Place the reserved potato slices on top. Return to the oven and bake for 25 minutes, or until lightly browned. Remove from the oven and let cool for 15 minutes. Cut into wedges and serve.

# Tuscan Torta with Spinach, Chard, and Raisins

This tart with a lattice top is a real showstopper. Your guests' eyes will light up when it's brought to the table. Known as a *torta rustica* in Italy, versions are served around Easter in celebration of the season. The filling is traditionally spinach, though I've incorporated other greens for more contrast in flavors. Other versions can have sausage, eggplant, and peppers as the filling.

MAKES ONE 9-INCH DOUBLE-CRUST TART; SERVES 8 AS A MAIN COURSE

DOUGH

1 package active dry yeast

1/2 teaspoon sugar

1 cup warm water (105° to 115°F)

1/4 cup olive oil

1 large egg, lightly beaten

1 teaspoon kosher salt

2 3/4 cups all-purpose flour, plus more for dusting

FILLING

2 bunches chard, coarsely chopped (including stems)

2 tablespoons unsalted butter

Kosher salt

2 bunches green onions, sliced 1/4 inch thick (including green parts)

4 cups packed spinach leaves, coarsely chopped

2 cups packed arugula leaves, coarsely chopped

1 bunch fresh flat-leaf parsley, stemmed

1/2 cup fresh basil leaves

1/2 cup golden raisins

Freshly ground black pepper

2 large eggs, beaten

1 cup whole-milk ricotta cheese, drained for 30 minutes

1/2 cup milk

1/2 cup shredded Gruyère cheese

1/4 cup grated pecorino cheese

1/4 teaspoon freshly grated nutmeg

Prepare a medium heat fire (375°F) in a wood-fired oven or cooker.

To make the dough, sprinkle the yeast and sugar over the water in a medium bowl and stir to dissolve the yeast. Let stand until foamy, about 5 minutes. Whisk in the oil, egg, and salt. Whisk in the flour 1/2 cup at a time until the dough is too stiff to work with a spoon. Turn the dough out onto a floured work surface and knead until smooth and elastic, about 4 minutes. Dust with flour as needed to keep the dough from sticking. To make the dough in a stand mixer fitted with a dough hook, combine the ingredients on low speed, then knead on high speed for 5 minutes.

Place the dough in an oiled bowl, turn to coat, and cover with a damp towel or plastic wrap. Let rise in a warm place until doubled in size, about 45 minutes.

To make the filling, chop the chard into bite-sized pieces. Melt the butter in a large skillet over medium heat on the floor of the wood-fired oven or on the stove top, then add the chard. Roast until the chard wilts and is tender, about 10 minutes. Lightly salt. Add a small amount of water if the pan is dry. Add the green onions, spinach, arugula, parsley, and basil, then lightly salt. Cook over medium heat until tender, about 5 minutes.

Add the raisins and salt and pepper to taste.

Reserve 2 tablespoons of the beaten eggs. Using a whisk, beat the remaining beaten eggs with the ricotta and milk in a large bowl until smooth. Stir in the cheeses, nutmeg, and the greens. Taste and adjust the seasoning.

On a lightly floured board, divide the dough into 2 pieces. Roll one piece out to an 11-inch round that is ⅛ inch thick. Fit the dough into a 9-inch springform tart pan that is 3 inches deep. Add the filling. Roll out the second piece of dough to the same thickness. Using a ravioli cutter, cut into ¾-inch-wide strips. Place the strips ½ inch apart across the surface of the tart, weaving alternate strips to create a lattice. Cut extra dough to 1 inch from the top of the pan. Fold the draped dough up over the strips, and crimp the edges with your fingers or a fork. Brush the lattice and rim with the reserved beaten egg.

Place on a baking sheet pan and bake for 25 to 30 minutes, or until golden brown. Let cool for 10 minutes on a wire rack, then remove the springform rim. Let cool for 20 to 30 minutes, then cut into wedges and serve.

# Wild Mushroom, Fennel, Chard, and Gruyère Tart

This tart has a crunchy cornmeal crust filled with an earthy combination of wood-roasted mushrooms and chard paired with caramelized fennel and nutty cheese. If chanterelles or oyster mushrooms aren't available, use all cremini mushrooms. The tart will still be sensational.

MAKES ONE 11-INCH TART; SERVES 8 AS A MAIN COURSE

CRUST

3/4 cup fine cornmeal

2 cups all-purpose flour

1 1/2 teaspoons salt

1/2 teaspoon sugar

7 tablespoons cold unsalted butter

2 tablespoons olive oil

8 to 10 tablespoons ice water

FILLING

1 fennel bulb, trimmed

4 large chard leaves, thick stems removed

1 teaspoon fennel seeds

1/4 cup olive oil

1 1/2 teaspoons kosher salt, plus more for seasoning

1/4 cup dry white wine

8 ounces mixed chanterelle and oyster mushrooms, stemmed

1/2 teaspoon freshly ground pepper, plus more for seasoning

1/4 teaspoon freshly grated nutmeg

2 large eggs

1 large egg yolk

1/2 cup milk

3/4 cup heavy cream

1 cup shredded Gruyère or Italian fontina cheese

Prepare a medium heat fire (375°F) in a wood-fired oven or cooker.

To make the crust, combine the cornmeal, flour, salt, and sugar in a food processor and pulse until mixed. Cut the butter into ½-inch cubes and add a few at a time to the processor, pulsing until the butter pieces are the size of a small pea. With the machine running, gradually add the olive oil until incorporated, then add 6 table-spoons of the ice water. If dough is still too dry to come together, add more water just until the dough pulls away from the sides of the bowl and forms a ball. Do not over-work the dough! Roll into a disk, wrap in plastic wrap, and refrigerate for at least 2 hours or overnight.

To make the filling, quarter the fennel bulb length-wise. Cut out and discard the core, then cut each quarter into ¼-inch-thick lengthwise slices. Cut the chard leaves into fine shreds. Slightly crush the fennel seeds with a large chef's knife or in a mortar.

Toss the sliced fennel in 2 tablespoons of the olive oil and ½ teaspoon salt. Spread on a rimmed baking sheet, add the white wine, and roast in the oven until ten-der and slightly caramelized, about 25 minutes. Tear the mushrooms lengthwise into bite-sized pieces. Toss with 3 tablespoons of the olive oil, ½ teaspoon salt, ½ teaspoon pepper, add the crushed fennel seeds, then repeat the roasting process as with the fennel.

Add the chard leaves to the roasted mushrooms, toss, and return to the oven to cook until the chard is wilted, 5 to 7 minutes. Remove from the heat and let cool. Add the nutmeg and lightly salt and pepper. Remove from the heat and set aside to cool slightly.

Increase oven or cooker temperature to 400°F. Roll the dough between 2 sheets of plastic wrap or parchment paper to a 13-inch-diameter round that is ⅛ inch thick. Fit the dough into an 11-inch tart pan with a removable bottom. Prick the dough with a fork on the bottom and sides and prebake for 12 minutes. Remove from the oven and let cool for 5 to 10 minutes before adding the filling.

Whisk together the eggs, egg yolk, milk, and cream, and ½ teaspoon salt in a bowl. Place the tart pan on a baking sheet. Line the prebaked shell with the mushroom-chard mixture and top with the roasted fennel. Sprinkle with half of the cheese, then pour the custard over the mixture. Top with the remaining cheese and bake until set and golden, 25 to 35 minutes. Let cool on a wire rack for 15 minutes. Remove from the tart pan, cut into wedges, and serve.

# Puff Pastry Pissaladière

A pissaladière is a crisp, flaky pizza-like pastry popular in the south of France. This version is made with prepared puff pastry, then topped with the traditional olives and anchovies. Here it is made as one rectangular tart, though you can make individual ones as well. The onions are roasted in the oven until soft, jammy, and a bit smoky. If you don't have oven-roasted tomatoes in your pantry, sun-dried tomatoes packed in olive oil can be substituted. My favorite element is the grated dried goat cheese at the end.

MAKES ONE 10- TO 11-INCH TART; SERVES 8 TO 10 AS A FIRST COURSE

MELTED ONIONS

1/4 cup olive oil

1 1/2 pounds yellow onions, cut into wedges 1/8 inch thick

3/4 cup white balsamic or Champagne vinegar

2 tablespoons sherry vinegar

Freshly ground white pepper

2 teaspoons sugar

2 teaspoons fresh thyme leaves


1 sheet frozen puff pastry, thawed in the refrigerator

1 large egg yolk beaten with 1 tablespoon heavy cream

1 cup Oven-Roasted Tomatoes (page 187), cut into
      narrow strips

4 cloves roasted or blanched garlic (page 192), minced

1/2 cup niçoise olives, pitted and sliced

2 tablespoons fresh thyme leaves

Kosher salt

Anchovy fillets, drained and soaked in milk (optional)

1/2 cup grated aged goat cheese, such as crottin

Prepare a medium heat fire (375°F) in a wood-fired oven or cooker.

To make the melted onions, heat the olive oil in a large skillet over medium heat and sauté the onions until translucent, about 7 minutes. Add the vinegars and a pinch of white pepper. Decrease the heat, stir in the sugar, and cook until the liquid is almost completely reduced and the onions have "melted" into a jam, 20 to 25 minutes. Remove from the heat. Stir in the thyme. Set aside.

Place the puff pastry on a floured surface and roll out 1 inch larger all around. Lay on a baking sheet lined with parchment. Cut 3/4-inch-wide strips off each side of the puff pastry. Brush the edges of the pastry with the yolk mixture and place the cut strips on the edges to make a pastry rim. Cover the inside evenly with the toppings, starting with the melted onions and ending with the anchovies. Brush the rim with the yolk mixture. Place on a grate in the oven and bake until golden brown, about 15 minutes.

Remove from the oven and immediately dust with the grated goat cheese. Cut into portions and serve warm.

# Milanese Risotto, Leek, and Asparagus Tart

This colorful tart uses leftover cooked risotto for the crust, in this case risotto milanese, the classic that is infused with saffron. Any leftover risotto you have can be frozen and saved for this purpose. You can cube pancetta and roast in the oven until rendered of fat and slightly crisp, then add that to the filling of the tart. Smoked poultry such as chicken or duck is great as well.

MAKES ONE 10-INCH TART; SERVES 8 AS A SIDE DISH

2 1/2 cups leftover risotto milanese or other risotto

1 3/4 cups Asiago or pecorino romano cheese, coarsely grated

5 tablespoons olive oil, plus more for coating

3 tablespoons fresh thyme leaves

12 to 14 stalks asparagus, trimmed, peeled, and cut into 4-inch pieces

Kosher salt

4 leeks (white part only), sliced lengthwise into eighths

Grated zest of 1/2 lemon

1/2 teaspoon freshly ground white pepper

3 large eggs, beaten

5 sprigs thyme

Prepare a medium heat fire (375°F) in a wood-fired oven or cooker.

Toss the risotto with 1 cup of the Asiago cheese. Heat 3 tablespoons of the olive oil in a 10-inch ovenproof skillet or clay casserole. Line the bottom and sides of the pan or dish with the risotto mixture and press to form a solid crust. Sprinkle with 1 tablespoon thyme leaves and coat with 1/2 cup of the cheese. Bake in the oven for 15 to 18 minutes, or until golden.

Lightly toss the asparagus in olive oil and salt, then roast on a baking sheet in the oven until slightly browned, about 15 minutes.

Slice the leeks crosswise into 1/4-inch slices and rinse well. Heat the remaining 2 tablespoons olive oil over medium heat in a skillet and sauté the leeks until soft, about 7 minutes. Lightly salt and set aside.

Line the baked crust with the remaining 2 tablespoons thyme leaves, the lemon zest, and sautéed leeks, and then arrange the asparagus in a starburst pattern. Lightly salt and add the pepper. Pour the eggs over the filling. Top with the remaining cheese and a fan of the thyme sprigs. Bake in the oven until the eggs are firm and the cheese has formed a golden brown crust, about 25 minutes.

Remove from the oven and let stand for 10 to 15 minutes. Turn out by placing a cutting board over the top, then flip over to turn the tart onto the cutting board. Place a large plate over the top of the tart and flip over again so the asparagus side is on top. Cut into wedges and serve warm.

# Rustic Corn, Tomato, and Basil Tart

This is the perfect tart to celebrate summer. It showcases the ripest heirloom tomatoes, fresh corn, and basil. You can use any tomatoes, but I like to use a mixture of colors. The corn kernels add crunch and a burst of flavor. The tang of the goat cheese pulls all the tastes together.

MAKES ONE 12-INCH TART; SERVES 8 AS A MAIN COURSE

1½ pounds yellow tomatoes, cut into ¼-inch-thick slices
1½ pounds red tomatoes, cut into ¼-inch-thick slices
Kosher salt

DOUGH
1 cup fresh corn kernels (about 2 ears)
1 tablespoon freshly squeezed lime juice
3 tablespoons fresh goat cheese, at room temperature
1½ cups all-purpose flour
¼ cup fine yellow cornmeal
½ teaspoon kosher salt
4 tablespoons cold unsalted butter, cut into cubes

FILLING
½ cup shredded fresh basil leaves
½ cup shredded Italian fontina cheese
1 tablespoon whole fresh oregano leaves, minced
4 tablespoons fresh bread crumbs
½ teaspoon kosher salt, plus more for seasoning
¼ teaspoon cracked black pepper
1 egg for wash
½ teaspoon coarse sea salt
¼ cup crumbled fresh goat cheese

Prepare a medium-hot fire (400°F) in a wood-fired oven or cooker.

Arrange the tomato slices in a single layer on paper towels and lightly salt. Let drain for 10 minutes, then gently squeeze to remove more juice.

To make the dough, combine ¾ cup of the corn, the juice, and goat cheese in a food processor and process until smooth. Combine the flour, cornmeal, and salt in a large bowl and stir with a whisk to blend. Cut in the butter with a pastry cutter until the mixture resembles coarse meal. Stir in the corn mixture and combine until a soft dough forms. Knead gently 3 or 4 times.

Place the dough on plastic wrap and cover with a second layer of plastic wrap. Press into a 6-inch disk. While still covered, roll the dough into a 14-inch round. Place on a parchment-lined baking sheet and refrigerate for 45 minutes or freeze for 10 minutes, until the dough is firm and the plastic wrap can be easily removed.

To make the filling, combine ¼ cup of the basil, the fontina, and oregano. In a separate bowl, combine 2 tablespoons of the bread crumbs and the ½ teaspoon kosher salt. Arrange the cheese mixture on the rolled-out dough, leaving a 1½-inch border. Dust with the bread-crumb mixture. Arrange half of the tomatoes, overlapping the slices, over the cheese. Sprinkle with the remaining corn kernels, lightly salt, and dust with the remaining bread crumbs. Arrange the second layer of tomatoes on top and sprinkle lightly with salt and the cracked black pepper.

Fold the edges of the dough toward the center, gently pleating like a galette; press to seal. Brush with egg wash and sprinkle with ½ teaspoon coarse sea salt. Bake in the oven for 20 minutes; remove and top the center with the crumbled goat cheese. Press the cheese lightly into the tomatoes. Return to the oven and bake for another 20 minutes, or until the crust is golden.

Remove from the oven and set aside for at least 20 minutes or up to 45 minutes. Sprinkle the tart with the remaining basil leaves; cut and serve at room temperature.

# Spinach, Mushroom, and Feta Pie

This phyllo pie is absolutely beautiful! I serve it often for brunch. It's a version of the Greek spanakopita, but with mushrooms and a more complex flavor. You can make this recipe into filled triangles for appetizers or small individual 4-inch tortes for a showy presentation. The bread crumbs between the layers of phyllo add a wonderful crunch.

**MAKES ONE 8-INCH TORTE; SERVES 8 AS A MAIN COURSE**

### SPINACH-ONION FILLING

2 tablespoons olive oil

1 bunch green onions, coarsely chopped, including some green parts

1 (10-ounce) package frozen spinach, thawed and drained

1/4 cup dry white wine

1 tablespoon capers, rinsed and drained

1/2 teaspoon kosher salt, plus more for seasoning

1/4 teaspoon freshly ground white pepper, plus more for seasoning

1 1/2 teaspoons minced fresh dill

6 ounces domestic feta, crumbled (rinsed if in brine)

8 ounces oyster mushrooms, torn into bite-sized pieces

8 ounces shiitake mushrooms, stemmed and chopped

1/4 cup olive oil

1/2 cup (1 stick) unsalted butter

1 cup toasted bread crumbs

1 tablespoon minced fresh dill leaves

1 teaspoon dried thyme

1/2 teaspoon sweet pimentón (Spanish smoked paprika)

Grated zest of 1 lemon

1 teaspoon salt

12 sheets frozen phyllo pastry, thawed in refrigerator

Prepare a medium heat fire (375°F) in a wood-fired oven or cooker. Brush an 8-inch springform pan with olive oil.

To make the filling, heat the olive oil in a sauté pan over medium heat and sauté the onions for 5 minutes. Add the spinach and sauté for another 5 minutes. Add the white wine and cook until the liquid is mostly evaporated. Add the capers, salt, and white pepper. Remove from the heat, stir in the dill, and let cool. Stir in the feta.

Sauté or oven-roast the mushrooms separately in 2 tablespoons of olive oil with a little salt until almost dry. Remove from the heat. Season with white pepper and more salt if needed. Set aside in separate bowls.

Melt the butter in a small saucepan over medium heat and stir in the remaining olive oil. Set aside and keep warm.

Combine the bread crumbs, dill, thyme, pimentón, zest, and salt in bowl. Set aside.

Lay the phyllo on a work space and cover with a kitchen towel, then damp paper towels.

On a cutting board, lay one pastry sheet lengthwise and, starting in the center, brush to the edges with the butter mixture. Generously sprinkle with the bread-crumb mixture. Cover with another sheet and brush with the butter mixture as before. Generously sprinkle with more of the bread-crumb mixture. Cover with a third sheet and brush again. Cut about 2 inches off one short side. Gently place the stacked sheets in the springform pan, pressing down to the bottom and draping the excess over the edges of the pan. Fill with the shiitake mushrooms.

Repeat the phyllo layering process with three more sheets of pastry, the butter mixture, and the bread crumbs. Cut about 2 inches off one short side. Gently place these sheets in the springform pan, pressing down over the mushrooms and draping the excess over the edges of the pan. Fill with half of the spinach-onion mixture.

Repeat the phyllo layering process and trimming again. Layer in the pan as before, and fill with the oyster mushrooms.

Repeat the phyllo layering process, trimming, and layering in the pan. Fill with the remaining spinach-onion mixture. Cover with the bread-crumb mixture. Fold all the excess draped phyllo into the center to cover the spinach-onion mixture and create the top crust.

Generously brush with the butter mixture and bake in the oven for 25 to 30 minutes, or until the top is golden and the crust is crisp. Remove from the oven and let cool for 15 minutes before removing from the springform pan. Cut into wedges and serve warm.

# CHAPTER 10

# Low & Slow:
# Braising to Barbecue

Fall apart, melt in your mouth, succulent, juicy—all of these words describe meats, poultry, fish, and even fruits and vegetables covered and cooked slowly at low temperatures. Low and slow cooking not only creates food with evocative complex flavors, but it emits intoxicating aromas in the process. Some of our most familiar home-cooked favorites, such as pulled pork, braised short ribs, and corned beef and cabbage, are cooked using low and slow methods that melt the fat or collagens in the meat and produce a crisp outer crust. Whether hot-smoked, poached, box pit–roasted, or braised, all of these methods employ moist heat environments for cooking in a wood-fired oven, cooker, smoker, or box roaster. Some recipes use milk, beer, or wine to transmit heat, while others use oil to poach. Even indirect heat from a grill can be used if the food being cooked is tightly covered and in the proper cookware. Simple, flavorful foods can be prepared using these methods with little maintenance on the part of the cook.

Here are some of my favorite traditional classics as well as more contemporary dishes using these methods.

# Low & Slow Guidelines

Here is a brief overview of the most common techniques used for low and slow cooking.

**Hot-smoking:** This method uses indirect heat and hot smoke at temperatures that actually cook the food (180° to 225°F). The food being cooked is kept uncovered in an enclosed environment to absorb the flavor of the smoke.

**Poaching:** This method of gently cooking food in liquid in a covered vessel at just below boiling point (212°F) can take place in salted water, vinegar water, stock, wine, sugar syrup, or olive oil. The liquid and amount of it depend on the food being cooked. The poaching liquid can often be utilized to flavor a sauce to accompany the food cooked in it. The most common foods for poaching are fish, eggs, poultry, and fruit.

**Box pit–roasting:** This form of roasting takes place in a moist sealed environment such as a Cuban box cooker. The heat source is contained above the box, not coming in contact with the food being cooked. The heat radiates down into the cooking chamber. Traditionally used to roast whole pigs or other meats, essentially, this is pit-cooking done above ground in a container. The food being cooked is typically brined (if meat or poultry) or marinated for added moisture, then cooked at chamber temperatures of 200° to 275°F. A probe thermometer is an essential tool to monitor the internal temperature of the meat, poultry, or fish.

Vegetables, fruits, and even grains can be pit-roasted. Some foods can take on more complex flavor if wrapped-cookery is employed using aromatic or edible leaves to contain and flavor the food being cooked.

**Braising:** This technique dates back to the earliest days of cooking when the braising pot was placed on embers or slid into the community bread oven at the end of the day's baking. Braising is an uncomplicated, low-maintenance method that demands little from the cook. Inexpensive cuts of meat can be transformed into tender, succulent food by this method of cooking. The low gentle heat melts the collagen (protein) in tougher cuts of meat and poultry, rendering them extremely tender. The natural gelatin in the meat contributes flavor-packed juices for making a delicious sauce. Even more tender foods such as vegetables, fish, and small cuts of meat can be braised. The foods are first browned, then simmered gently with a small amount of liquid (water, wine, or stock) in a closed vessel, melding with their own juices, to produce rich, aromatic, complex flavors (temperatures typically range between 300° and 325°F). Opening the vessel to reduce liquids for the last few minutes creates an even deeper layer of flavors, especially in a wood-fired environment.

# Succulent Smoked Salmon

This was the first dish I learned to cook on the Big Green Egg, at the masterful hands of Ray Lampe, aka Dr. BBQ. This recipe yields a very succulent, lightly cooked, smoky fish. It calls for salmon, but any seasonal fish such as halibut or even trout can be substituted. I like to keep the seasoning to a minimum so the flavor of the fresh fish comes through. If you choose to add more herbs to your version, dried herbs work best. Adding fruit wood chips to the hot coals contributes another layer of flavor. I like apple wood best for maintaining a sweet flavor. Serve with lightly dressed baby greens.

**SERVES 8 TO 10 AS AN APPETIZER OR A FIRST COURSE**

1 (2-pound) salmon fillet, skin on, pin bones removed

1 tablespoon or so coarse sea salt, or as needed

1 teaspoon coarsely ground juniper berries (optional)

2 tablespoons minced fresh dill, for garnish

2 tablespoons capers, for garnish

Prepare the Big Green Egg or wood-fired grill for indirect cooking.

In the case of the BGE, use a plate setter with the legs up and grate in place to separate the fish from the heat source. If you like, soak 1 cup of apple wood chips in water for 30 minutes, then sprinkle them over the charcoal 10 minutes after lighting. Close the lid of the BGE and open the top vents and the bottom vents ½ inch.

To cook on a wood-fired grill, place a pizza stone over the fire, then place 2 fire brick pavers on opposite sides of the pizza stone, about 8 inches apart. Close the lid and open lower vents to ½ inch.

After 2 minutes, lay the salmon fillet on a perforated pizza pan or aluminum mesh pizza screen. Season with the sea salt and juniper berries and place on the grate. If using a grill, balance the pizza pan or screen on the fire brick pavers. Close the lid and smoke for 30 to 35 minutes at 190°F, or until the flesh is slightly firm to the touch but still looks moist. The color of the flesh should only be slightly lighter than when it started smoking. Remember, you are smoking the fish, not roasting it.

Check the doneness of the fish at the thickest section, using a fork to slightly pull away some of the flesh. It should be very moist and uniform in color. The color will have changed only slightly from when it was put on the fire.

Remove from the cooker or grill and let cool slightly. Slice thinly to serve; remove with a fish fork or a knife, leaving the skin behind. Store leftover fish on the skin; wrap in plastic and refrigerate for up to 1 week. Serve garnished with the dill and capers.

# Olive Oil–Poached Tuna with Fennel, Orange, and Olive Salad

Olive oil is very good as a poaching liquid, especially when you want the poaching liquid to gently transfer heat yet not penetrate the food. This method yields amazingly moist fish. And it's lovely to use the infused oil in the salad dressing for the accompanying salad.

### SERVES 4 AS A MAIN COURSE

1½ pounds center-cut albacore tuna or yellowtail

Fine sea salt, for rubbing

4 cloves garlic, cut into thick slices

1 bay leaf

2 teaspoons capers, drained and rinsed

4 strips orange zest

2 fennel bulb fronds

⅛ teaspoon white peppercorns

Olive oil to cover (about 3 cups)

### SALAD

1 small fennel bulb, trimmed, cored thinly sliced lengthwise

½ cup picholine olives, pitted and coarsely chopped

1 orange, peeled and segmented, juice reserved

2 teaspoons herbes de Provence

3 tablespoons coarsely chopped fresh flat-leaf parsley

Kosher salt and freshly ground black pepper

### DRESSING

¼ cup reserved poaching oil (from Olive Oil–Poached Tuna)

3 tablespoons Champagne vinegar

Kosher salt

2 cups baby arugula

2 tablespoons chopped fresh flat-leaf parsley, for garnish

Sea salt, for dusting

Prepare a low heat fire (190° to 210°F) in a wood-fired oven or cooker and use a grate to prepare for cooking with indirect heat.

Rinse the tuna and pat dry. Rub sea salt on all sides and let stand at room temperature for 1 hour.

Choose an 8-inch glazed earthenware baking dish that the fish fits snugly into. Add the garlic, bay leaf, capers, orange zest, fennel fronds, and white peppercorns to the dish. Place the tuna on top and add enough olive oil to cover. Cover tightly with aluminum foil. Place on a grate in the oven or in a covered cooker over indirect heat to poach for 45 to 55 minutes, until cooked through.

Meanwhile, combine all the ingredients for the salad, adding salt and pepper to taste. Set aside at room temperature.

Test the fish for doneness after 35 minutes; it should be firm to the touch on the outside and still pink on the inside. Remove from the heat and let cool for 5 minutes. Drain the fish, reserving the olive oil, and break or cut it into serving-size pieces.

To make the dressing, whisk 3 to 4 tablespoons of the poaching olive oil into the vinegar and dress the salad. Taste and adjust the seasoning.

Arrange the arugula on each plate, top with pieces of the poached fish, and then spoon on the salad. Garnish with the parsley and dust with sea salt.

# Wine-Poached Shrimp with Smoky Tomato Sauce

Poaching refers to cooking in a liquid that's heated to just below boiling. The shells are kept on the shrimp while cooking to keep them tender and to allow the shells to release their flavor into the poaching liquid. Cooking halibut, salmon, or shellfish this way produces a delicate texture.

**SERVES 6 AS AN APPETIZER**

18 large shrimp in the shell, scored down the back and deveined

2 cups dry white wine

2 cups light vegetable or shrimp stock

2 cloves garlic, peeled

$1/2$ teaspoon fennel seeds

$1^1/2$ teaspoons kosher salt

Smoky Tomato Sauce (recipe follows)

Prepare a low-medium heat fire (225°F) in a wood-fired oven or cooker.

Combine the wine and stock in a saucepan and warm slightly. Put the shrimp in a shallow baking dish, then cover with the wine and stock. Add the garlic, fennel, and salt to the liquid, then cover tightly and bake for 15 to 20 minutes, until the shrimp are evenly pink.

Remove the shrimp from the liquid and let cool slightly, then remove the shells. Return the dish to the oven and cook to reduce the liquid by one-third. Reserve $1/4$ cup of it for the sauce. Toss the shrimp in the remainder of the reduced liquid just before serving.

## SMOKY TOMATO SAUCE

**MAKES ABOUT 3$1/2$ CUPS**

4 tomatoes, seeded and halved

2 unpeeled shallots, halved

$3/4$ cup olive oil

Kosher salt

$1/2$ teaspoon freshly ground black pepper

$1/4$ cup reduced poaching liquid (from Wine-Poached Shrimp)

Juice of 1 lemon

2 tablespoons white balsamic vinegar

Freshly ground white pepper

1 cup chopped fresh basil leaves

$1/4$ cup chopped fresh mint leaves

Prepare a medium-hot fire (400°F) in a wood-fired grill. Or, if poaching the shrimp in an oven, cook the tomatoes and shallots there as well. Place them on a grate or a grill pan to mark and cook as directed.

Combine the tomatoes, shallots, 3 tablespoons of the olive oil, salt, and the black pepper in a bowl and toss to coat. Grill the tomatoes and shallots, cut side down, for 15 minutes, or until they are softened and the skins have shriveled. Remove from the grill and spread on a baking sheet to cool to the touch. Remove the tomato skins and shallot peels, then chop the vegetables. Combine in a bowl along with any juices and set aside.

Whisk the poaching liquid, lemon juice, and vinegar together in a bowl. Gradually whisk in the remaining $1/2$ cup olive oil to make an emulsion. Stir into the tomato mixture and add salt and white pepper to taste. Stir in the chopped herbs. Set aside for 20 minutes for the flavors to come together. Serve as a dip for the shrimp.

# Beer-Braised Short Ribs

This is a wood-fired version of a recipe from my Sonoma-chef friend, John McReynolds. Braising short ribs in a wood-fired environment creates amazing rich flavors and succulent meat. Of course, these short ribs can be made in a conventional oven and they will still be lovely. Serve with spaetzle, mashed potatoes, or plain buttered noodles.

SERVES 4 AS A MAIN COURSE

3 pounds short ribs, cut into 2-inch pieces with the bone attached

Kosher salt and freshly ground black pepper

2 teaspoons olive oil

2 large onions, sliced

2 carrots, peeled and chopped

1 stalk celery, chopped

2 cloves garlic, peeled

2 Roma tomatoes, chopped

1 teaspoon caraway seeds

2 teaspoons sweet Hungarian paprika

1 (12-ounce) bottle dark beer

2 cups rich chicken or beef stock, plus more as needed

8 sprigs thyme

2 bay leaves

Prepare a medium-hot fire (400°F) in a wood-fired oven or cooker.

Pat dry the short ribs. Rub salt evenly over the meat and sprinkle with pepper. Heat the olive oil in a large, heavy roasting pan or clay baker over medium-high heat on a grill or on the floor of a wood-fired oven. Add the meat and brown evenly on all sides. Transfer the short ribs to a large plate and set aside.

Add the onions, carrots, celery, and garlic to the roasting pan. Bake in the oven for about 20 minutes, stirring 2 or 3 times, until the vegetables are soft and lightly browned. Add the tomatoes, caraway seeds, paprika, beer, the 2 cups stock, the thyme, and bay leaves, stirring to scrape up the browned bits from the bottom of the pan. Return the short ribs to the pan, cover, and bake in the cooler front area of the oven until fork-tender, about 2½ hours, checking to add more stock or water if needed. Uncover the short ribs and bake for 30 minutes to caramelize the meat and reduce the liquid.

Carefully transfer the short ribs to a platter and cover with aluminum foil. Pour the braising liquid from the pan through a sieve and press lightly on the cooked vegetables with the back of a large spoon to release more liquid. Discard the vegetables. Pour the liquid into a small saucepan, bring to a boil, and skim the fat off the top. Continue gently boiling and skimming until all of the fat is removed and the sauce is reduced to desired thickness.

The bones may be left in the short ribs or removed before serving.

# Lone Star Barbecued Brisket

A fatty, tough cut of meat, brisket becomes a thing of beauty through long, slow smoking, as in this recipe adapted from *The Big Book of Outdoor Cooking & Entertaining* by Cheryl and Bill Jamison. Brisket should shed a lot of weight during cooking, which can only be accomplished fully in a wood-burning pit or similar homemade smoker. The Jamisons' cut of preference is a full packer-trimmed brisket, which is the full cut with a thick layer of fat on one side.

SERVES 12 TO 18 AS A MAIN COURSE

RUB

3/4 cup sweet Hungarian paprika

1/4 cup freshly ground black pepper

1/4 cup coarse sea salt or kosher salt

1/4 cup sugar

2 tablespoons chili powder

2 tablespoons garlic powder

2 tablespoons onion powder

2 teaspoons cayenne pepper

1 (10- to 12-pound) packer-trimmed beef brisket

BEER MOP

1 (12-ounce) can or bottle of ale beer

1/2 cup cider vinegar

4 tablespoons canola oil

2 tablespoons Worcestershire sauce

1/2 onion, slivered, or 2 to 4 garlic cloves, minced

1 tablespoon Rub (above)

1 1/2 teaspoons coarsely ground pepper

Pickled jalapeno slices, fresh jalapeno slices, Tabasco sauce, or other hot sauce (optional)

1/2 cup water

REAL TEXAS BRISKET SAUCE (OPTIONAL)

1 1/2 cups barbecued brisket drippings from sliced brisket (above), supplemented with bacon drippings if needed

2 teaspoons Worcestershire sauce

1 teaspoon cayenne pepper

The night before you plan to barbecue, combine all the rub ingredients in a small bowl and stir to blend. Reserve 1 tablespoon of the rub for the mop. Apply the rest of the rub evenly to the brisket, massaging it in well. Place the brisket in a large self-sealing plastic bag and refrigerate overnight.

Before you begin to barbecue, remove the brisket from the refrigerator and let sit, uncovered, at room temperature for 45 minutes. Fire up the smoker, bringing the temperature to 180° to 220°F.

To make the mop, combine all the ingredients in a saucepan and warm over low heat.

Transfer the brisket to the smoker, fat side up, so the juices will help baste the meat. Cook until very tender, 10 to 16 hours, 60 to 75 minutes per pound of brisket. Every hour or so, baste the blackening hunk with the mop.

Remove the meat from the smoker and let stand at room temperature for 20 to 30 minutes. Cut the fatty top section away from the leaner bottom portion. An easily identifiable layer of fat separates the two areas. Trim the excess fat from both pieces and slice both pieces thinly against the grain. Watch as you work though, because the grain changes direction. Collect all the meat drippings as you cut.

To make the sauce, combine all the ingredients in a bowl and use a bit of sauce to moisten the meat; serve the rest alongside.

# Slow-Roasted Split Turkey with Citrus-Chile Glaze

This dish got me hooked on the La Caja China box roaster, which was introduced to me by Tom Romano, who along with his wife, Linda Gilbert, owns Broadway Catering in Sonoma, California. They use the La Caja a lot at home and for catered events. The guests are always awestruck with this mysterious box roaster and its fabulous results. The sauce is Tom's nod to the flavors of the Caribbean, where the La Caja is from.

SERVES 8 TO 10 AS A MAIN COURSE

1 half turkey, about 6 pounds

BRINE (OPTIONAL)
8 cups water
2/3 cup salt
2/3 cup sugar

CAJA TURKEY RUB
1 cup olive oil
2 tablespoons pimentón (Spanish smoked paprika)
1/3 cup packed light brown sugar
1 tablespoon onion powder
Pinch of chipotle chile powder
6 cloves garlic, minced
1/2 tablespoon cumin seeds, toasted and ground
1 tablespoon kosher salt
1/2 tablespoon freshly ground black pepper

CITRUS-CHILE GLAZE
2 tablespoons olive oil
1 tablespoon minced garlic
1 tablespoon cascabel chile powder
1/4 cup light corn syrup
1/4 cup orange blossom honey
1/4 cup ponzu sauce, or 2 tablespoons *each* freshly squeezed
        lime juice and lemon juice
2 tablespoons freshly squeezed lime juice
2 tablespoons freshly squeezed orange juice

To brine the turkey, combine all the brine ingredients in a large nonreactive container and submerge the turkey completely. Refrigerate for at least 4 to 6 hours or overnight. Rinse and let come to room temperature.

To make the rub, combine all the rub ingredients in a bowl. Rub the split turkey generously with the rub and set aside at room temperature for 30 minutes.

To make the glaze, heat the olive oil in a saucepan over medium heat and sauté the garlic for 30 seconds. Add the chile powder and sauté for 30 more seconds. Increase the heat, add the remaining ingredients, and cook until reduced to a light syrup. Strain and let cool to room temperature.

Place the turkey, skin side up, in the La Caja China box roaster on a rack over a drip pan. Cover with the lid, add the charwood, and light.

If you are roasting this turkey in a Big Green Egg or wood-fired oven, prepare a medium-hot fire (325°F) and roast covered, on a rack.

After 1 hour, remove the lid, turn the turkey over, cover again, add more charwood as needed, and cook for 15 minutes. Remove the lid and brush both sides of the turkey with the glaze. Place a probe thermometer into the turkey breast, return the lid, and roast until the thermometer registers 170° to 175°F. Remove from the heat and set aside on a baking sheet. Brush again with the glaze and let rest for about 20 minutes. Carve and serve.

# Milk-Braised Pork with Mushroom-Artichoke Ragù

Braising meat in milk is a classic cooking technique in Italy. The milk acts as a tenderizer and creates a beautiful caramelized sauce. This is a perfect dish for the wood-fired oven or cooker because the braising pot is surrounded on all sides by heat and cooks more evenly. When artichokes aren't in season, use leeks or even Swiss chard in their place.

**SERVES 6 AS A MAIN COURSE**

1 (3- to 4-pound) boneless pork shoulder, some fat trimmed

Kosher salt and freshly ground black pepper

3 tablespoons olive oil

2 onions, coarsely chopped

3 juniper berries, crushed

2 bay leaves

2 sprigs rosemary or savory

2 cloves garlic, thinly sliced

3 1/2 cups whole milk

MUSHROOM-ARTICHOKE RAGÙ

3 tablespoons olive oil

2 pounds mushrooms (chanterelles, cremini, or shiitakes),
    sliced (if using shiitakes, stem them first)

1 1/2 cups fresh or thawed frozen artichoke hearts

3 cloves garlic, thinly sliced

1 cup dry white wine

1 teaspoon kosher salt

1/2 teaspoon freshly ground black pepper

Grated zest of 1 lemon

1/4 teaspoon freshly ground nutmeg

1/2 cup walnuts, toasted and chopped

Prepare a medium fire (325°F) in a wood-fired oven or cooker.

Season the pork with salt and pepper. Heat the olive oil in a Dutch oven or heavy casserole over medium-high heat until it starts to shimmer. Add the pork and sear all over until well browned. Transfer the pork to a plate and set aside. Remove all but 3 tablespoons of fat from the pot. Return the pot to medium heat and add the onions, juniper berries, bay leaves, and rosemary and cook until the onions are tender, about 5 minutes. Add the garlic and continue to cook until the garlic is lightly golden, about 3 minutes. Return the pork to the pot and pour in the milk. Cover and place in the oven to braise for 2 hours, turning the pork 2 or 3 times during the course of cooking.

Meanwhile, to make the ragù, heat the olive oil in a small Dutch oven or heavy casserole over medium heat until it shimmers. Add the mushrooms and artichoke hearts, cover, and place in the oven to cook for 15 minutes. Uncover and add the garlic, wine, salt, and pepper. Cover and return to the oven for 10 minutes, stirring a few times while cooking. Uncover and cook until the artichoke hearts are tender and some of the juices have evaporated, about 15 minutes. Remove from the oven and stir in the lemon zest. Taste and adjust the seasoning. Set aside and keep warm.

Uncover the pork after 2 hours and cook for 30 minutes, or until the meat is fork-tender. Transfer the roast to a plate and tent with aluminum foil.

Remove the bay leaves, rosemary, and juniper berries from the milky sauce. Skim any excess fat from the top. The milk will have curdled in the cooking process. Using an immersion blender, process the sauce until smooth. Add the nutmeg and walnuts. Return to the oven to heat through. Taste and adjust the seasoning.

Slice the meat and serve with the sauce spooned over the top. Accompany with the ragù.

# Lamb Braised in Yogurt with Onions and Tomatoes

This is a braised version of a traditional Turkish kebab dish. It's adapted from one of my favorite cookbooks, *Classical Turkish Cooking: Traditional Turkish Food for the American Kitchen* by Ayla Algar. The meat is marinated in yogurt and lemon juice overnight to ensure tenderness. A separate yogurt sauce is used to braise the lamb. The result is very tender meat in a rich, flavorful sauce. Cooking in a wood-fired oven adds a slight smokiness and depth to the onions and tomatoes. Serve this with couscous or rice pilaf.

SERVES 4 AS A MAIN COURSE

2¹/₂ pounds boneless lamb stew meat, cut into 1-inch cubes

MARINADE
1 cup plain whole-milk yogurt
Juice of 1 lemon
1 teaspoon cumin seeds
¹/₂ teaspoon salt

4 tablespoons olive oil, plus more for rubbing
Kosher salt and freshly ground black pepper
3 large unpeeled cloves garlic
5 large ripe tomatoes
2 poblano or large jalapeno chiles
1 pound white onions, shredded (4 cups)
1 tablespoon cumin seeds
Pinch of red pepper flakes
1 teaspoon ground allspice
¹/₂ teaspoon ground ginger
Splash of red wine vinegar
3 cups chicken stock
5 cups whole-milk yogurt, drained overnight through
    a fine-mesh sieve
5 teaspoons cornstarch
Chopped fresh flat-leaf parsley, for garnish

Put the lamb in a large self-sealing plastic bag. Combine all the ingredients for the marinade and add to the bag. Marinate the lamb for 2 hours at room temperature or overnight in the refrigerator. If refrigerated, let come to room temperature for 30 minutes before proceeding.

Prepare a medium heat fire (325°F) in a wood-fired oven or cooker.

Drain the meat and pat dry. Rub it with olive oil and dust with salt and pepper.

Roast the garlic, tomatoes, and poblano chiles in a dry cast-iron skillet over high heat until the skins are toasted and blistered. Transfer to a plate and let cool to the touch. Peel and seed the tomatoes and chiles. Finely chop all.

Heat the olive oil in a nonreactive skillet over medium heat until it shimmers. Add the onions, cumin, red pepper flakes, allspice, and ginger and sauté for 5 minutes. Add the chopped vegetables and vinegar, then place the lamb on top of the mixture. Add 1½ cups of the stock. Spoon some of the onion mixture over the lamb. Cover tightly with a lid or aluminum foil and place in the oven to cook for 45 minutes, or until the vegetables have melted slightly.

In a separate bowl, combine the drained yogurt and cornstarch. Stir the remaining stock and the drained yogurt mixture into the lamb. Cover and return to the oven to cook for another 30 minutes, or until the lamb is fork-tender. The sauce will look curdled at this point. Transfer the lamb to a plate and use a hand blender to smooth the sauce, then return to medium heat, uncovered, to thicken, about 15 minutes. Add the braised lamb, cover with some of the sauce and return to the oven, uncovered, to heat through.

Serve the lamb hot over couscous, topped with the sauce and garnished with parsley.

NOTE

To stabilize the yogurt to prevent curdling when heated, stir in 1 teaspoon of cornstarch per 1 cup of yogurt. Also, make sure the yogurt is at room temperature before heating.

# Provençal Chicken

This recipe was inspired by the flavors and aromas of Provence. The combination of herbes de Provence, picholine olives, and rosé wine transports me there each time I make this dish! The honey and prunes add just the right amount of sweetness. The chicken is cooked on the bone for more flavor. This dish can also feature duck beautifully. Of course, it tastes even better when served with a glass of the same dry rosé.

### SERVES 6 AS A MAIN COURSE

1 cup toasted bread crumbs or panko (Japanese bread crumbs), finely ground

2 teaspoons herbes de Provence

1 teaspoon kosher salt, plus more for seasoning

1/2 teaspoon freshly ground black pepper, plus more for seasoning

3 bone-in chicken breasts, halved crosswise

3 bone-in chicken thighs, halved crosswise

1/4 cup olive oil

6 shallots, peeled and halved

8 unpeeled cloves garlic

12 pitted prunes

3 tablespoons picholine or other green olives with pits

1 tablespoon capers, drained and rinsed

1 tablespoon fennel seeds

1 cup dry rosé or white wine

1 tablespoon honey

1 orange, cut into 6 wedges, juice reserved

Prepare a medium heat fire (325°F) in a wood-fired oven or cooker. If using a wood-fired oven, keep a small fire (one small log) going in the far left rear of the oven to maintain the heat throughout the cooking process.

Combine the bread crumbs, herbes de Provence, the 1 teaspoon salt, and the 1/2 teaspoon pepper in a bowl. Pat the chicken dry, then toss in the bread-crumb mixture, and set aside on a baking sheet.

Heat the olive oil in a large cast-iron skillet or shallow clay baking dish over medium heat and brown the chicken on all sides. Transfer the chicken to a shallow clay baking dish or ceramic-coated cast-iron cookware. Add the shallots, garlic, prunes, olives, capers, and fennel seeds. Combine the wine and honey plus any reserved orange juice and pour the liquid over the chicken. Add more salt and pepper. Cover tightly with a heavy ovenproof lid or aluminum foil and bake in the oven for 45 minutes, or until the chicken is tender and the mixture is bubbly. Uncover and place the orange wedges, skin side up, around the chicken, then cook for another 15 minutes to caramelize the chicken. Remove from the oven and let rest for 10 minutes before serving.

# Clambake in a Box

This version of a classic clambake was designed a La Caja China box roaster. If you don't have one, use a large stockpot layered with 4 inches of seaweed, then loaded and cooked as directed, using a wood-fired grill or a wood-fired oven. Cover and cook for about 1 hour, then remove the lid and cook until tender. Note: You'll need about 5 pounds (1 gallon) of seaweed for this recipe.

### SERVES 20 AS A MAIN COURSE

6 chicken halves, refrigerated overnight in brine
    (see page 150)

4 dozen clams, scrubbed

3 pounds potatoes, scrubbed

20 ears corn, husks on, silks removed

Hot crusty bread, for serving

2 cups (4 sticks) unsalted butter, melted, for dunking

Line the bottom of a La Caja China box roaster with 6 to 8 inches of seaweed. Set the pig rack on top and place the chicken on one side of the rack. Insert a probe thermometer into the chicken breast. Put the charcoal lid and grate in place and light the charcoal. Roast for 1 hour.

Make a sack of burlap or double layers of cheesecloth to hold all the clams. Remove the lid of the box and set the sack on the rack next to the chicken but not touching. Place one or two perforated pizza pans or screens on the other side of the chicken and add the potatoes and corn. Cover all with another thin layer of seaweed. Replace the lid and add another layer of charcoal as directed. Roast for 45 minutes, or until the probe thermometer registers 175°F. Check the potatoes for doneness. Remove the lid and let steam release for about 15 minutes.

Serve directly from the box, or line a platter with seaweed, arrange the food on it, and serve. Serve with hot crusty bread and melted butter for dunking.

# Overnight Beef Chili Colorado

Bruce Aidells is a big fan of wood-fired cooking. Because a wood-burning oven has the ability to hold heat for long periods, it's ideal for long, slow cooking overnight. Chili has become such a popular American classic that there are chili cookoffs and festivals held all over the country. Chili con carne has its origins in the slow-cooked stews from Mexico. One such stew, chili colorado, was no doubt made in clay pots and cooked overnight in the village baker's oven. In this recipe the ingredients are just combined and cooked slowly over a long period of time.

SERVES 8 TO 10 AS A MAIN COURSE, WITH LEFTOVERS

6 dried ancho chiles

6 slices bacon, diced

1 large onion, chopped (2 cups)

5 pounds beef brisket, trimmed and cut into 3-inch cubes

Kosher salt, for seasoning, plus 1 teaspoon

Freshly ground black pepper

1 habanero chile, stemmed and seeded (optional)

6 cloves garlic, peeled

2 teaspoons cumin seeds

1 teaspoon dried oregano

1 teaspoon ground coriander

2 tablespoons chili powder

1 (14½-ounce) can fire-roasted diced tomatoes with
        green chiles

1 (12-ounce) bottle Mexican beer

Chopped stems from 1 bunch cilantro

4 mild green chiles, fire-roasted, peeled, seeded, and diced,
        or 1 (7-ounce) can diced fire-roasted green chiles

GARNISHES

½ cup fresh cilantro leaves

1 cup finely chopped sweet red onion

One sliced avocado

Shredded Monterey Jack cheese

Warm corn or flour tortillas, for serving

Tear the ancho chiles apart. Discard the seeds and stems and place the chiles in a bowl. Pour boiling water over to cover and soak for at least 30 minutes or up to several hours.

Prepare a medium heat fire (350°F) in a wood-fired oven.

Fry the bacon in a large Dutch oven over medium heat until it begins to brown. Add the onion and sauté for 5 minutes. Season the meat with salt and pepper to taste. Remove the pot from the heat and stir in the meat.

Place the soaked chiles and about ½ cup of the soaking liquid in a blender (save the remaining liquid to add to the pot later if needed). Add the habanero, garlic, cumin, oregano, coriander, the 1 teaspoon kosher salt, and the chili powder. Blend to form a puree and pour over the meat along with the tomatoes, beer, cilantro stems, and green chiles. Stir well to coat the meat and blend the ingredients. Cover pot and place in the oven. Place the door on the oven to retain heat and leave the chili overnight or up to 12 hours, until the meat is fork-tender.

Remove the pot from the oven. Skim the excess fat from the surface of the chili, or chill in the refrigerator overnight and remove the congealed fat. Season to taste with salt and pepper. Reheat the chili over low heat. Serve in bowls with the garnishes on the side and warmed tortillas to roll and dip.

# Wood-Smoked Cheese Fondue

Fondue is traditionally made tableside in a stainless steel or ceramic pot over a small open flame. Here is my smoke-infused version of a classic fondue using a wood-fired oven or the indirect heat of a grill or cooker. My favorite way of making the fondue is in a clay sand pot as used in Asian cooking. These pots are inexpensive and fun to cook with (see Resources). You can use a ceramic pot with a lid as well. Or, for a dramatic presentation, place the fondue pot on the table over a small charcoal hibachi to keep hot (see Resources). You can use endive or radicchio leaves and red peppers for dipping in addition to the bread. Serve with a small, simple salad.

SERVES 6 TO 8 AS A MAIN COURSE

2½ cups dry white wine

6 cloves garlic, thinly sliced

1½ tablespoons cornstarch

1 tablespoon water

3 cups shredded Gruyère cheese

3 cups shredded Italian fontina cheese

3 tablespoons Kirsch liqueur (optional)

¼ teaspoon freshly grated nutmeg

Kosher salt

1 (1-pound) loaf artisan bread, such as a bâtard or
      pugliese, ends removed, cut into bite-sized cubes

Prepare a medium heat fire (325°F) in a wood-fired oven or cooker.

Combine the wine and garlic in a small clay or enameled cast-iron pot with a lid. Cover and place in the oven to cook until the garlic is soft, about 20 minutes. Uncover and continue to bake for 10 minutes, or until the garlic has melted. Remove from the oven and mash the garlic. Make a slurry of the cornstarch and water and stir into the mixture to thicken. Stir in the cheeses and return to the oven to melt them, removing to stir a few times. Add the optional Kirsch, the nutmeg, and salt to taste, then stir to combine. Add a little water if the sauce has reduced too much. Remove from the oven and place on a tabletop burner or hibachi to keep hot.

Each person should have a fondue fork and a small plate. Place a piece of the bread on a fondue fork, swirl in the fondue, and bring up and twirl the bread to remove the excess cheese.

# Braised Cauliflower, Potato, and Onion Curry

This lovely vegetable curry uses traditional Indian spices and coconut milk. It is best made in a clay pot in a wood-fired oven or cooker. If you don't have or don't care for coconut milk, replace it with whole-milk yogurt. The finished dish will be less sweet but still very good. Serve it with rice to accompany chicken or fish.

**SERVES 4 AS A SIDE DISH**

3 tablespoons canola oil

2 onions, chopped

1/2 jalapeno chile, seeded and minced

3/4-inch piece fresh ginger, peeled and minced

4 cloves garlic, minced

1 teaspoon brown mustard seeds

1/2 teaspoon cumin seeds

1 1/2 teaspoons coriander seeds

2 whole cloves

4 whole peppercorns

1 teaspoon kosher salt

1/2 teaspoon ground turmeric

1/2 teaspoon Indian (hot) paprika

1 1/2 cups coconut milk

1/2 cup water

1 pound potatoes, peeled and cut into large pieces

1 head cauliflower (2 pounds), broken into bite-sized florets

Prepare a medium heat fire (325°F) in a wood-fired oven or cooker.

Heat 2 tablespoons of the oil in a small skillet over medium heat and sauté the onions until translucent, 3 minutes. Add the jalapeno and ginger and cook for 2 minutes. Stir in the garlic and cook for another 2 minutes. Set aside.

Heat the remaining 1 tablespoon oil in a glazed clay pot over medium heat and sauté the mustard seeds, cumin, coriander, cloves, and peppercorns until fragrant. Remove the spices and reserve the pan.

Combine the onion mixture, sautéed spices, salt, turmeric, and paprika in a blender. With the machine running, pour in 1 cup of the coconut milk or enough to create a thin paste.

Place the paste in the reserved glazed clay pot used for the spices and thin with the water. Stir in the potatoes, cover, and place in the oven for 7 minutes. The potatoes should be partially cooked at this time. Add the cauliflower and the remaining coconut milk. Add more water if needed to thin. Cover and return to the oven until the vegetables are tender and the flavors have blended, about 20 minutes. Uncover and bake for another 5 minutes so the food will absorb some of the flavor of the wood. Serve hot or at room temperature.

# CHAPTER 11

# Wood-Fired Sweets and Desserts

This collection of my favorite wood-fired sweets features items for breakfast and dessert, all of which benefit from being cooked in a wood-fired environment. Even dessert pizzas can be easily prepared using live fire. If you don't have a wood-fired oven, use a pizza stone or granite piastra on a grill grate over a live wood fire to cook over indirect heat, mimicking an oven environment.

# Apple-Prune Galette

Fran Gage is a wonderful pastry and bread maker as well as a cookbook author. She shares her special recipe for a marvelous fruit tart here. It is simple to make and quite delicious with its classic French apple and prune filling. Fran's recipe for a sweet crust is wonderful and can be used for other fruit tarts.

MAKES ONE 12-INCH GALETTE; SERVES 8 TO 10

DOUGH

1¼ cups unbleached all-purpose flour

½ teaspoon fine sea salt

3 tablespoons sugar

9 tablespoons cold unsalted butter, cut into small pieces

4 tablespoons cold water

FILLING

6 or 7 pitted prunes, coarsely chopped

1 pound flavorful baking apples, such as Gravenstein
     or Braeburn

2 tablespoons sugar

2 tablespoons Calvados, Armagnac, or Cognac

1 tablespoon sugar, for sprinkling

Prepare a hot fire (450°F) in a wood-fired oven or cooker.

To make the dough, combine the flour, salt, and sugar in a bowl. Stir with a whisk to blend. Using your fingertips or a pastry blender, rub or cut the butter into the flour until some of the butter is in flakes and the rest is the size of peas.

Stir in the water 1 tablespoon at a time to moisten the dry ingredients. Form the dough into a ball. It will still look a little rough with some streaks of butter. On a floured board, divide the dough into 2 pieces, flatten each piece into a disk, and wrap in plastic. Refrigerate for at least 1 hour or up to 3 days. Freeze the extra disk of dough for up to 1 month.

To make the filling, cover the prunes with hot water and let soak for 15 minutes. While the prunes soak, peel and core the apples and cut them into ⅛-inch slices. Drain the prunes. Put them in a bowl with the apples and toss with the sugar and liquor.

On a floured board, roll 1 disk of the dough out into a 14-inch round. Transfer the disk to a cornmeal-dusted pizza peel. Mound the fruit in the middle, leaving a 2-inch border of exposed dough. Fold the dough over the fruit, pleating it to close as you go around. Sprinkle the folded-over dough with the 1 tablespoon of sugar.

Slide the galette from the peel directly onto the hearth of the wood-fired oven. Bake until the crust is brown and the apples yield to the tip of a knife, 25 to 30 minutes.

# Apricot Tart with Lavender Crème Anglaise

This is one of my favorite desserts. Dried apricots, almonds, and honey are the key sweet flavors of the Mediterranean. With a nod to Provence, we top it all with Lavender Crème Anglaise.

MAKES ONE 10-INCH TART; SERVES 8

PASTRY DOUGH

2¼ cups all-purpose flour

⅓ cup almond flour or finely ground almonds

2 tablespoons sugar

½ teaspoon finely grated nutmeg

1 teaspoon salt

¾ cup (1½ sticks) cold unsalted butter, cut into small pieces

½ cup ice water

FILLING

12 ounces dried California or Turkish apricots

¼ cup amaretto or Grand Marnier liqueur

2½ cups water

¾ cup orange marmalade plus 2 tablespoons water

¼ cup turbinado sugar

½ cup sliced almonds

Lavendar Crème Anglaise (recipe follows)

Prepare a medium heat fire (350°F) in a wood-fired oven or cooker.

To make the dough, combine the dry ingredients in a large bowl or food processor. Using your fingertips or a pastry blender, rub or cut in the butter until it is the size of peas. Gradually stir in half of the ice water until the dough comes together in a ball. Add a bit more water only if needed. Do not overwork the dough. On a floured board, form the dough into a disk, cover with plastic wrap, and refrigerate for 30 minutes or overnight.

To make the filling, combine the apricots, amaretto, and water in a small saucepan and cook over low heat until the apricots are plump and soft, about 20 minutes. Remove from the heat, drain, and set aside.

Roll out the dough on a lightly floured board to a 12-inch round about ⅛ inch thick. Fit into a 10-inch tart pan with a removable bottom. Run a rolling pin over the top to remove the excess dough.

Fit a sheet of parchment paper in the tart shell and fill it with pie weights or dried beans. Place the pan in the oven and prebake for 15 minutes. Remove from the oven and let cool for 10 minutes before filling.

Increase the oven heat to 375°F by adding a small log to the fire. Cover the crust with the apricots, fanning the fruit and overlapping each slice by ½ inch. Heat the orange marmalade and water over low heat to a spreadable consistency. Spread over the apricots. Sprinkle with the turbinado sugar, then top with the almonds.

Place on a baking sheet and bake in the oven for 20 to 30 minutes, until golden. Remove from the oven and let cool for at least 15 minutes. Once cool, remove from the tart pan, portion, and serve topped with the crème anglaise.

# LAVENDER CRÈME ANGLAISE

## MAKES ABOUT 4 CUPS

2 cups heavy cream

1 cup half-and-half

1/3 cup finely ground Lavender Sugar (see note)

1/3 cup wildflower honey

2 tablespoons dried lavender buds

4 large egg yolks

Combine the cream, half-and-half, sugar, and honey in a nonreactive saucepan. Heat over medium-low heat to just below the boiling point, stirring with rubber spatula or wooden spoon to dissolve the sugar and honey. Remove from the heat and add the lavender. Cover and let steep for 10 minutes.

Pour the mixture through a fine-mesh sieve into a bowl, pressing the lavender with the back of a large spoon to release the liquid. Discard the lavender. Return the flavored cream to the saucepan.

Place the pan over medium-low heat and reheat to just below the boiling point. Whisk the egg yolks in a small bowl. Gradually whisk about 1 cup of the hot cream into the yolks to temper the eggs. Add the mixture to the saucepan with the remaining cream and cook, stirring constantly, until the custard thickens and coats the back of a wooden spoon. Do not let the mixture boil, or the eggs will curdle.

Remove from the heat and pour through a fine-mesh sieve into a large stainless steel bowl. Stir the custard gently for a few minutes to cool slightly. Cover with plastic wrap pressed directly onto the surface of the custard and refrigerate until ready to serve. It can be kept overnight.

## LAVENDER SUGAR

To make lavender sugar, combine 1 cup sugar and 1 teaspoon dried lavender in a glass jar and let stand for 1 day. Grind in a spice grinder before using.

# Breakfast Focaccia with Grapes and Figs

Focaccia can be either savory or sweet. Topped with grapes, figs, and candied orange peel, it's a great breakfast or brunch bread. This is one of the favorites from my cooking classes. You can substitute the grapes and figs with other fresh fruit such as strawberries and peaches. Keep the toppings light; don't overload the focaccia.

MAKES ONE 12 BY 17-INCH FOCACCIA

DOUGH

1 tablespoon active dry yeast

2 cups warm water (105° to 115°F)

1/2 cup olive oil

2 teaspoons kosher salt

4 cups all-purpose flour

TOPPING

4 tablespoons blood orange olive oil (see note)

1 tablespoon minced fresh rosemary

2 tablespoons vanilla turbinado sugar (see note)

1/2 cup red seedless grapes, halved

1/2 cup figs, quartered

1/4 cup Candied Orange Peel (recipe follows)

To make the dough, sprinkle the yeast over the warm water in a large bowl. Stir to dissolve the yeast and let stand until foamy, about 5 minutes. Stir in 1/4 cup of the olive oil and the salt. Whisk, then stir in the flour 1/2 cup at a time to make a soft dough.

Turn the dough out onto a lightly floured board and form it into a ball. Put the dough in a lightly oiled large bowl, turning the dough to coat it with oil. Cover the bowl with a damp towel or plastic wrap and let rise in a warm place until doubled in size, 1 to 1 1/2 hours.

Prepare a medium-hot fire (425°F) in a wood-fired oven or cooker.

Lightly oil a 12 by 17-inch baking sheet. Place the dough on the pan and stretch to cover as much of the pan as possible. Dimple the top and stretch again. Cover with a towel and set aside to rest for 15 minutes.

Brush the dough with 3 tablespoons of the orange olive oil and sprinkle on the rosemary and 1 tablespoon of the vanilla turbinado sugar. Gently press the grapes, figs, and candied orange peel into the dough. Dimple the dough again. Cover with a towel to rest for another 15 minutes.

Sprinkle on the remaining vanilla turbinado sugar and place in the oven. Bake until golden brown, 20 to 25 minutes. Remove from the oven and drizzle with the remaining orange olive oil. Place on a wire rack to cool for 10 minutes, then remove from the baking sheet to further cool. Cut into serving-size squares or rectangles and serve.

# CANDIED ORANGE PEEL

MAKES ABOUT 1 CUP

1 orange, scrubbed
1 cup simple syrup
1/2 cup sugar

Using a vegetable peeler, remove the zest and part of the white pith from the fruit in strips. Cut the peel into 1/8-inch-wide strips. Place in a nonreactive saucepan and cover with the simple syrup. Bring to a low simmer and cook for 15 minutes. Drain and spread on a parchment-lined baking sheet. Toss with the sugar and leave out uncovered overnight to let dry.

Place in an airtight jar with half of the sugar. Reserve the remaining citrus oil–infused sugar in a separate jar for future use as a garnish or as flavored sugar.

## CITRUS OLIVE OILS

Some condiment olive oils are a combination of two fruits, the olive and a citrus fruit, that have been pressed together. The process allows all the essential oils of the citrus to join with the oil of the olives. My favorite ones are from the Olive Press in Sonoma, California (see Resources). These finishing oils are wonderful as a baking ingredient, a dressing ingredient, in a marinade, or as a finishing oil simply drizzled over grilled fish or tossed onto plain pasta. They will transform the simplest of foods. Try the Meyer lemon, blood orange, and clementine oils (see Resources).

## VANILLA TURBINADO SUGAR

Turbinado sugar is a natural raw cane sugar that has not been bleached or over-processed. It is the result of slowly boiling layer upon layer of sugarcane, which allows the golden chunky crystals to retain their natural molasses and richness of flavor. Use it as an ingredient (especially to sweeten whipped cream) or sprinkle it on cookies or pie crusts. To make vanilla turbinado sugar, place a used vanilla bean pod or two in a jar of turbinado sugar and let stand for about 1 week to infuse the sugar with the vanilla flavor.

# Roasted Pear-Apple Crostata

For those who love to make simple seasonal fruit desserts, making a rustic tart is one of the most enjoyable ways of creating a beautiful dessert. A proper dough is important, but the overall shape created for the actual tart is up to you. In this recipe for an Italian tart, the pears and apples are first roasted until lightly caramelized, which increases their flavor.

MAKES ONE 12-INCH TART; SERVES 8

### PASTRY DOUGH
2½ cups all-purpose flour, plus more for dusting

¼ cup almond flour or almond meal

3 tablespoons sugar

½ teaspoon freshly grated nutmeg

1½ teaspoons salt

¾ cup (1½ sticks) cold unsalted butter, cut into
   small pieces

⅓ to 1 cup ice water

### FILLING
2 large apples, peeled, cored, and each cut into 10 wedges

3 pears, peeled, cored, and each cut into 8 wedges

¼ cup Muscat or other dessert wine

2 tablespoons turbinado sugar (see page 167), plus more
   for sprinkling

½ cup apple jelly

½ cup sliced almonds

Whipped crème fraîche or mascarpone cheese, for serving

Prepare a medium heat fire (375°F) in a wood-fired oven with a baking stone. Leave a small fire (one small log) off to left rear of the oven when ready to bake.

To make the dough, combine all of the dry ingredients in a large bowl and stir with a whisk to blend. Using your fingertips or a pastry blender, cut or rub in the butter until the pieces are the size of a pea. Gradually stir in ⅓ cup of the ice water, then more if needed until the dough comes together and forms a ball. Do not overwork the dough. On a lightly floured board, form the dough into a 1-inch-thick disk, cover with plastic wrap, and refrigerate for at least 30 minutes or overnight.

To make the filling, toss the apples and pears with the Muscat and sugar and place on a baking sheet. Place on the floor of the oven and roast for about 10 minutes, until the fruit is lightly softened and caramelized. Remove from the oven and set aside to cool slightly. Pour any juices from the baking sheet into a small bowl and set aside.

Lightly dust the dough with flour and roll out between sheets of parchment paper to a 12-inch round about ⅛ inch thick. Warm the apple jelly over low heat to make spreadable. Add up to 2 tablespoons of the reserved roasted fruit juices. Spread one-third of the jelly on the bottom of the crust, leaving a 1½-inch border. Again leaving a border, cover the pastry with the roasted fruit, fanning and overlapping each slice slightly. Top with the almonds, then drizzle the remainder of the jelly over the top. Fold the edges of the dough up toward the center, pleating as you go. Sprinkle the entire crostata with more turbinado sugar. Slide the parchment and tart onto a large baking sheet or pizza pan and bake in the oven for 25 to 30 minutes, until the crust is golden on the top and bottom.

Remove from the oven and let cool for at least 15 minutes. Cut into wedges and serve warm, topped with whipped crème fraîche or mascarpone.

# Grilled Dessert Pizza with Pears, Figs, and Honey Mascarpone

Pizza makes a fun dessert, and this one can be served for breakfast as well. It's topped with seasonal fruit and a dollop of honey-flavored mascarpone cheese, but you can serve it with vanilla bean ice cream instead, if you prefer. Try other grilled fruits such as peaches or nectarines on this pizza.

MAKES 4 SMALL PIZZAS; SERVES 8

4 pears, peeled, cored, and cut into $1/2$-inch slices

6 large firm fresh figs, halved lengthwise

3 tablespoons balsamic vinegar

2 tablespoons turbinado sugar (see page 167), plus more
   for sprinkling

$1/4$ cup chestnut or other honey

8 ounces mascarpone cheese

Grated zest of 1 orange

Basic Pizza Dough (page 33)

Blood orange or clementine olive oil (see page 167),
   for brushing

Prepare a medium-hot fire (425° to 450°F) in a wood-fired grill.

Place the pears and figs in a bowl and gently toss with the balsamic vinegar. Grill the pears until marked but not charred on both sides. Lightly grill the cut sides of the figs. Remove from the heat and toss with the 2 tablespoons turbinado sugar, then set aside to cool slightly. Cut the fruit into bite-sized pieces if desired.

Combine the honey and mascarpone in a small bowl. Stir in the orange zest and set aside.

Flour a wood pizza peel; shape each dough ball into an 8- or 10-inch round on the peel. Lightly brush the top of the rounds with olive oil. Take to the grill and flip the rounds, oiled side down onto the grill. Cover and cook until puffed and marked from the grill, about 5 minutes. Turn over, brush with orange olive oil, and top sparingly with the pears and figs. Sprinkle more turbinado sugar over the tops of the pizzas, including the edges. Cook for 5 minutes, until the crust is golden.

Let cool for 5 minutes, then cut into wedges and serve topped with the mascarpone mixture.

# Grilled Fruit with Lemon Zabaglione

This is a very simple dessert that anyone can master. Bananas, pineapple, and stone fruit that is firm and not too ripe are best in this recipe. Grilled fruit also make a great salad (toss in some beautiful cherries or grapes). It's also wonderful at breakfast served with yogurt and granola. And it makes a fabulous chutney when combined with raisins, juice, and Indian spices (see page 190). So, when you grill fruit, grill some extra to make these other dishes.

SERVES 6

1/3 cup packed brown sugar or maple syrup

Juice of 2 oranges

2 nectarines or peaches, halved and pitted

3 plums, halved and pitted

2 bananas, halved lengthwise

1 pineapple, peeled, cored, and cut into chunks

Lemon Zabaglione (recipe follows)

Fresh mint leaves, for garnish

Prepare a medium-hot fire (425° to 450°F) in a wood-fired grill.

Stir the sugar into the orange juice until dissolved. Brush the cut fruit with the sugar mixture.

Grill the fruit, cut side down, for about 5 minutes, or until the fruit is slightly soft and well marked. Move to indirect heat and continue to cook to the desired softness. Remove from the heat and set aside to cool.

Slice the fruit and keep each kind in a separate bowl. Let stand at room temperature for 30 minutes to allow flavors to mix.

Portion an assortment of the fruits into 6 bowls. Top with the zabaglione and garnish with mint leaves.

## LEMON ZABAGLIONE

MAKES ABOUT 6 CUPS

2 large eggs

4 large egg yolks

1/2 cup sugar

Grated zest of 2 lemons

Juice of 1 lemon

1/3 cup Muscat or other dessert wine

Combine all the ingredients in a stainless steel bowl and set aside.

Choose a saucepan large enough to set the bowl over and fill it with 2 inches of water. Bring to a simmer.

Whisk the egg mixture in the bowl. Place the bowl over the simmering water and whisk vigorously until it is about triple in volume and thick and frothy. Lift the bowl off the steam a few times, while whisking, to insure that the mixture does not get too hot and scramble the eggs. The total cooking time will be about 8 minutes. Remove the bowl from the heat and whisk to cool slightly. Serve now, or cover with plastic wrap pressed directly onto the surface and use within 2 hours. It may need to be whisked again just before serving.

# Grilled Polenta Cake with Berries and Cream

Many dense cakes such as pound cake can be grilled with great success. The grilling lightly toasts the cake and adds depth to the flavor. Here, Joanne Weir shares her favorite Mediterranean version, grilled polenta cake topped with seasonal berries tossed in a fruit sauce. Note: Make the cake a day in advance, and the berry compote several hours in advance so the flavors have time to blend.

SERVES 8

### CAKE

1/4 cup sliced almonds

3/4 cup all-purpose flour

1/2 cup finely ground polenta

1 1/2 teaspoons baking powder

1/8 teaspoon salt

8 1/2 tablespoons unsalted butter, at room temperature

1 cup sugar

3 large eggs, at room temperature

3 large egg yolks, at room temperature

1 teaspoon vanilla extract

### FRUIT COMPOTE

4 cups mixed fresh berries

1 (8-ounce) package frozen raspberries, thawed

2 tablespoons sugar

2 tablespoons water

Melted butter, for brushing

Confectioners' sugar, for dusting

Whipped cream, for topping

Prepare a medium heat fire (350°F) in a wood-fired oven or cooker. Generously butter an 8-inch loaf pan.

To make the cake, put the almonds in a heavy, self-sealing plastic bag and crush them into small pieces using a rolling pin. Dust the buttered loaf pan with the almonds, tilting the pan to coat all sides.

Sift the flour, polenta, baking powder, and salt together. Cream the butter and sugar together in an electric mixer until light and fluffy, 3 to 5 minutes. In a separate bowl, stir together the eggs, egg yolks, and vanilla extract. With the mixer running, very slowly add the egg mixture a little at a time until the eggs are completely incorporated. Stir in the dry ingredients until just incorporated, but do not overmix. Transfer to the prepared loaf pan and bake until the center is set, 30 to 40 minutes.

Prepare a hot fire (475°F) in a wood-fired grill.

To make the compote, gently toss the fresh berries in a bowl. In a blender or food processor, combine the raspberries, sugar, and water. Blend until smooth. Strain through a fine-mesh sieve. Pour half of the raspberry sauce over the mixed berries and toss together gently. Reserve the remaining raspberry sauce.

Cut the pound cake into 3/4-inch-thick slices. Brush each side with melted butter. Grill the slices until golden, about 1 minute per side.

To serve, spread two tablespoons of the reserved raspberry sauce on the bottom of each plate and place a slice of pound cake on top. Top with the berries and dust with confectioners' sugar. Top with a dollop of whipped cream if you wish. Serve immediately.

# Roasted Pineapple with Rum-Maple Glaze

This dessert is so simple, yet so tasty. It's fun to do at a campfire or in a backyard fire pit. Once the pineapple is secured to the spit with prongs, all you need to do is baste it with the rum syrup every few minutes until it's beautifully golden. The aromas from the syrup and the caramelizing pineapple are mouthwatering! Serve it with a slice of pound cake or, better still, with ice cream.

SERVES 6

1/3 cup maple or agave syrup

1/4 cup dark rum

Juice of 1 lime

1 pineapple, peeled

1 lime, cut into wedges

Place a rotisserie over a hot fire (425° to 450°F) in a wood-fired fire pit, grill, or campfire. Let the coals of the fire burn down to a glow.

Combine the maple syrup, rum, and lime juice in a small bowl. Skewer the pineapple with the spit rod and secure with the spit's prongs. Using a basting brush, coat the pineapple with the glaze. Place the spit 6 inches over the coals and roast, basting with the glaze every 5 minutes or so at first, less often as the pineapple roasts and colors. Roast until the pineapple is caramelized and the exterior is slightly soft to the touch, 25 to 35 minutes. Remove from the rotisserie and let cool for 10 minutes on the spit rod. Remove from the rod, slice or cut into chunks, slather on some more basting syrup, and serve with the lime wedges.

# Heirloom Tarte Tatin with Late-Harvest Riesling Sabayon

Tarte Tatin is a French upside-down apple tart named for the two sisters who invented the dish. This version is topped with puff pastry and baked in a wood-fired oven or by indirect heat on a grill. It can be topped with slightly sweetened whipped cream, or better still with a frothy sabayon infused with an aromatic late-harvest Riesling. The sabayon is also terrific on its own or with berries. Choose a good baking or pie apple such as Gala, Pink Lady, Gravenstein, Braeburn, or Jonathan.

MAKES ONE 10-INCH TART; SERVES 6

1 sheet puff pastry, thawed in the refrigerator
6 large heirloom apples
Freshly squeezed lemon juice, for brushing
1/2 cup (1 stick) unsalted butter
1/2 cup sugar
Late-Harvest Riesling Sabayon (recipe follows)

Prepare a medium heat fire (375°F) in a wood-fired oven or cooker, or prepare a wood-fired grill for cooking over indirect heat.

Lay the pastry sheet on a work surface and cut it into an 11-inch round. Cover the pastry with a damp towel so it doesn't dry out.

Peel and core the apples and cut them into sixths. Brush with lemon juice so they do not brown.

Melt the butter and sugar together in a 10-inch cast-iron skillet and cook over low heat until the sugar dissolves. Arrange the apples in the sugar mixture in a snug, even pattern cut side down. Place on the stove top or on the grill over low to medium heat and cook for about 20 minutes until the apples are slightly soft and the sugar has begun to caramelize.

Place the puff pastry round securely on top of the apples and tuck down inside the edge of the pan. Prick with a fork or cut a vent in the top.

Bake in the oven or over indirect heat in a covered grill for 15 to 20 minutes, until the pastry is golden brown.

Set aside to cool for 10 minutes, then place a serving dish over the pan and turn it upside down to unmold. The crust will have absorbed some of the juices. Cut into wedges and serve warm, topped with the sabayon.

## LATE-HARVEST RIESLING SABAYON

SERVES 6

2 large eggs
4 large egg yolks
1/2 cup sugar
1/3 cup late-harvest Riesling (or other sweet dessert wine)

Combine all the ingredients in a stainless steel bowl.

Choose a saucepan large enough to set the bowl over and fill it with 2 inches of water. Bring to a simmer.

Whisk the egg mixture in the bowl. Place the bowl over the simmering water and whisk vigorously until it is about triple in volume and thick and frothy. Lift the bowl off the steam a few times, while whisking, to insure that the mixture does not get too hot and scramble the eggs. The total cooking time will be about 8 minutes. Remove the bowl from the heat and whisk to cool slightly. Serve now, or cover with plastic wrap pressed directly onto the surface and use within 2 hours. It may need to be whisked again just before serving.

# Warm Apple and Sweet Potato Upside-Down Cake with Caramel Sauce

This dessert captures all the smells and tastes of fall. Similar to its cousin, pineapple upside-down cake, it is easily prepared in a cast-iron skillet, then turned out on a plate along with its syrup. Sweet potatoes serve as a binder and sweetener in this cake. Serve it with a dollop of tangy crème fraîche or a little warm caramel sauce.

MAKES ONE 10-INCH CAKE; SERVES 10 TO 12

5 tablespoons unsalted butter

3/4 cup packed dark brown sugar

2 large baking apples (such as Granny Smith, Braeburn, or Jonathan), peeled, cored, and each cut into 8 wedges

BATTER

5 tablespoons unsalted butter, at room temperature

1/2 cup packed dark brown sugar

1/2 cup granulated sugar

1 teaspoon vanilla extract

1 1/2 cups mashed cooked sweet potatoes (such as garnet yams)

2 large eggs

1 1/4 cups all-purpose flour

1/2 teaspoons baking soda

1 teaspoon baking powder

1/2 teaspoon kosher salt

1 1/2 teaspoons ground cinnamon

1 teaspoon ground ginger

1/2 teaspoon ground cardamom

1/4 teaspoon freshly grated nutmeg

3/4 cup buttermilk

Crème fraîche or warm Cinnamon-Caramel Sauce (page 179), for serving

Prepare a medium heat fire (350°F) in a wood-fired oven, or in a cooker or grill prepared for cooking with indirect heat.

Melt the butter in a 10-inch cast-iron skillet. Stir in the brown sugar. Arrange the apple sections in a circular pattern, rounded side down, on top of the sugar. Use the last section of the apple to fill the center. Bake in the oven or on indirect heat in a covered grill for 15 minutes. At this point, the apples should be half-submerged in the syrup and very soft.

While the apples are baking, prepare the batter. Beat the butter and sugars together in a stand mixer until fluffy and smooth. Beat in the vanilla, sweet potatoes, and then the eggs, one at a time, until smooth.

Sift the flour, baking soda, baking powder, salt, and spices into a separate bowl. Add this dry mixture to the batter in thirds until it is incorporated. Pour in the buttermilk and beat the batter on medium speed for 1 minute. Pour the batter over the hot apples and their syrup. Bake in the oven or over indirect heat in a cooker or grill for 35 to 40 minutes, or until the cake is golden and springs back when you push on the center.

Let the cake cool for 5 to 7 minutes, then unmold it onto a large flat platter or plate with a well. Let stand for 10 to 15 minutes to soak up the syrup. Cut into wedges and serve slightly warm, with a dollop of crème fraîche or a drizzle of warm caramel sauce.

# Blackberry Grunt

This is John Ash's recipe for a fun and easy one-dish dessert. Although there is some debate on what makes a "grunt," the definition seems to be that grunts, which are also called slumps, are simmered rather than baked in the oven. They are usually made with berries and the name supposedly comes from the sound the berries make as they simmer!

SERVES 6 TO 8

8 cups fresh or thawed frozen unsweetened blackberries

3/4 cup sugar, or as needed

1/2 cup dry red wine or water

1 tablespoon grated lemon zest

DOUGH

1 cup all-purpose flour

2 tablespoons sugar

1 teaspoon baking powder

1/2 teaspoon baking soda

1/8 teaspoon salt

2 tablespoons unsalted butter, melted

2/3 cup buttermilk (or a mixture of plain yogurt and skim milk or water), plus more as needed

2 tablespoons sugar mixed with 1 teaspoon ground cinnamon

Whipped cream, vanilla ice cream, crème fraîche, or sweetened yogurt, for serving

Prepare a medium heat fire (350° to 375°F) in a wood-fired oven, or in a cooker, grill, or campfire prepared for cooking with indirect heat.

Combine the berries, sugar, wine, and zest in a heavy, deep casserole and bring to a simmer over medium heat in a wood-fired oven or over indirect heat on a wood-fired cooker, grill, or campfire.

Meanwhile, make the dough by stirring the flour, sugar, baking powder, baking soda, and salt with a whisk in a bowl. Stir in the melted butter. Stir in enough buttermilk to form a soft, wet dough.

Using a soup spoon, place heaping spoonfuls of the dough on top of the fruit. Make sure you have at least one per person. Sprinkle the dumplings with the cinnamon sugar. Tightly cover with a lid or a sheet of aluminum foil and simmer over medium-low heat until the dumplings are puffed and set, about 12 minutes.

To serve, spoon the warm grunt into serving bowls and spoon on the topping of your choice.

# Warm Chocolate-Chipotle Cakes with Cinnamon-Caramel Sauce

This dessert is always a hit in my cooking classes. The combination of chocolate, cinnamon, and smoky chipotle often appears in Southwest American and Mexican cuisine, and the flavors marry beautifully in a wood-fired cooking environment. If you want a bit more heat, add more chile paste. You can also add a touch of chile powder to the Cinnamon-Caramel Sauce.

SERVES 8

4 dried chipotle chiles

6 tablespoons unsweetened prune juice

1/2 cup sugar

10 ounces bittersweet chocolate, finely chopped

3/4 cup (1 1/2 sticks) unsalted butter

4 large eggs

2 tablespoons all-purpose flour

1 teaspoon freshly-ground cinnamon (preferably Mexican canela)

1/8 teaspoon kosher salt

Cinnamon-Caramel Sauce (recipe follows)

Prepare a medium heat fire (350°F) in a wood-fired oven or cooker. Butter eight 4-ounce ramekins and dust with sugar, knocking out the excess sugar.

In the wood-fired oven or cooker, toast the chiles in a dry skillet, turning as they toast, for about 2 minutes. Discard the stems, seeds, and ribs, then soak the chiles in hot water to cover until softened, about 30 minutes. Drain, reserving the soaking liquid.

Puree the drained chiles in a food processor or blender, adding enough soaking liquid to form a paste. Force the paste through a fine-mesh sieve into a bowl and discard the solids. Set aside 1 1/2 tablespoons of the chile paste and freeze the remainder for another use.

Bring the prune juice and sugar to a boil in a medium saucepan, stirring until the sugar is dissolved. Pour the hot sugar syrup over the chocolate in a large bowl, stirring until the chocolate is melted. You may need to place it over a simmering water bath to melt completely. Add the butter and stir until melted. Whisk in the eggs, one at a time, then stir in the 1 1/2 tablespoons chile paste, the flour, cinnamon, and salt.

Place the ramekins in a baking pan; divide the batter among the sugar-lined ramekins and place in the oven or cooker. Fill the pan with 1/2 inch hot water and bake, uncovered, until the cakes are firm and crusted, 30 to 35 minutes. Check after 20 minutes for doneness, as each oven is different. The cakes need to be moist, not dry.

If using a Big Green Egg, put the plate setter in place with the grate on top, creating an oven. Place the sheet pan on the grate, fill with hot water, and close the lid.

Transfer the ramekins to a wire rack and let cool for 5 minutes. Unmold the warm cakes directly onto serving plates, crusty top side up. Drizzle with the caramel sauce and serve.

# CINNAMON-CARAMEL SAUCE

MAKES 1¹/₂ CUPS

2 cups sugar

¹/₂ cup water

2 teaspoons freshly ground cinnamon (preferably
    Mexican canela)

1¹/₂ cups heavy cream

Combine the sugar and water in a heavy saucepan. Cook over medium-low heat until the sugar dissolves. Increase the heat to medium-high; boil without stirring until the syrup becomes a deep amber color, occasionally brushing down the sides of the pan with a wet pastry brush and swirling the pan. Remove from the heat. Stir in the ground cinnamon until completely combined. Gradually add the cream and stir over low heat until the sauce is smooth. Remove from the heat and let stand until cool and pourable, about 30 minutes.

Store in a plastic squeeze bottle and use immediately or refrigerate for up to 1 month.

# CHAPTER 12

# Wood-Fired Pantry Basics

Preserving food by means of smoking and curing has been a worldwide practice for thousands of years. Today, these methods are used to impart color and a depth of flavor to food that cannot be achieved by other means.

A well-stocked pantry is a treasure trove of seasonal foods that a cook can use to create memorable meals. Hand-crafted pantry ingredients will dramatically enhance your recipes and spark your senses with ingredients preserved at the height of their flavor. Live-fire cooking techniques will allow you to create unique pantry basics to have on hand anytime you want to add their special flavors to your meals.

Why buy sun-dried tomatoes in a store when you can make a wood- roasted or dried version that is packed with more explosive flavor than any commercial product? When you make these and other basic ingredients yourself, you'll save money and enjoy yourself at the same time. Costly and exotic pantry foods will soon be replaced by your own handcrafted gems.

Home-crafted smoked and infused salts, smoked salmon, slow-roasted tomato paste, infused olive oils, tasty grilled chutneys, and spit-roasted chiles—all are easy to prepare over a wood fire. And creating then restocking a pantry allows wood-fired cooks to utilize the residual energy of their wood-fired cooker to the fullest. As the appliance cools, you can take advantage of the waning heat to create wonderful pre-served goods.

# Pantry Guidelines

Here are general guidelines for creating your wood-fired pantry followed by recipes for my favorite pantry staples. Let your imagination and the season's bounty be your guide. You'll have fun experimenting and discovering new ways to expand your culinary repertoire through the use of wood fire. Here are my recommendations for the best wood-fire preserving methods for fruits, vegetables, and herbs, as well as meats and cheeses.

## Fruits, Vegetables, and Herbs

When selecting produce to preserve, choose unsprayed, freshly picked fruits, vegetables, or herbs at the peak of their growing season.

### FRUITS

- To grill for chutneys, salsas, sauces, and jams: Pineapples, mangos, papayas, apples, bananas, pears, peaches, plums

- To oven-roast for chutneys, salsas, sauces, and jams: Pineapples, apples, bananas, pears, peaches, plums, any citrus

- To dry for pies, cobblers, and snacks: Pineapples, mangos, papayas, apples, pears, peaches, plums, strawberries, blueberries, cherries, grapes

### VEGETABLES

- To grill: All except those with very thin skins, or individual leafy greens

- To oven-roast: Root vegetables, tomatoes, broccoli, cauliflower, Brussels sprouts, mushrooms, squash, cabbage, celery, onions, garlic, artichokes, radicchio, endive

- To dry: Tomatoes, mushrooms, beans, peas, artichokes, peppers, carrots, celery, onions, garlic

- To spit-roast: All peppers, Roma tomatoes, corn on the cob, marinated mushrooms, potato wedges, quartered parboiled artichokes, Brussels sprouts

- To smoke: All peppers, onions, tomatoes, mushrooms, and sweet potatoes

## Drying

Wood-fired oven or cooker drying is easy and adds more depth of flavor than sun-drying. Drying prevents food spoilage by removing 80 to 90 percent of the food's water content.

### DRYING FRUITS AND VEGETABLES

1. Clean the food by washing in cold water to remove any dirt.

2. Core or pit, then quickly blanch in boiling water, drain, and pat dry.

3. Remove the skin and thinly slice the flesh for even drying.

4. Place sheets of metal mesh or pizza screens between each fire brick of a two-row stack. The bottom rack should be kept 6 to 8 inches from the heat source (oven floor or bottom fuel).

5. Spread the cut fruit or vegetables on the mesh without touching and in a single layer.

6. Using a wood-fired oven or cooker, maintain temperatures between 125° and 140°F, which allows moisture to be released while drying. For very thinly sliced vegetable chips or shoestrings, dry at 170°F degrees for 6 to 8 hours. For thicker-cut fruits and vegetables, dry for 12 to 18 hours, until 80 to 90 percent of the water content is removed.

Rotate drying racks periodically for more even temperature distribution.

7. Dry at the designated temperature until the desired texture is achieved. Let cool completely. After drying, fruits should be leathery, while vegetables should be bitter or crisp.

8. Store in airtight containers to keep moisture out. Eat dry or rehydrate as needed.

## Fruit Leather

Using about 1¹/₂ pounds of almost any fruit, puree in a blender along with ³/₄ cup sugar until smooth, then strain through a fine-mesh sieve. Place in an ovenproof nonreactive dish and place in a preheated 300° to 325°F oven. Bring to a boil, then move to lower heat and cook for about 45 minutes, or until the puree has reduced by half and is thickened. As the oven cools to 200°F, spread the puree over silicone baking mats and spread thinly using an offset spatula. Place in baking sheets over racks in the oven to dry until tacky, about 3 hours. Remove from the oven to cool on a wire rack until completely dry, up to 24 hours. Place a sheet of parchment over the leather, peel the leather off the silicone, and roll up in the parchment. Store in a sealed bag in a cool place for up to 1 month.

### DRYING HERBS

The lower temperatures (around 140°F) of a cooling wood-fired appliance may be used to dry herbs. Some of the flavor from the oven will be imparted to the herbs in the drying process. The appliance is effective because it provides a dry, warm environment in which the herbs can slowly dry in gentle heat. Branches or stalks of rosemary, thyme, oregano, marjoram, savory, basil, parsley, and dill are best. Loose fresh herb leaves and chives can also be dried.

1. Wash the herbs in cold water and pat dry. Spread out on a baking sheet and place in an oven or enclosed cooking environment such as a grill with a lid at 140°F for 45 minutes.

2. If using branches or sprigs, after 45 minutes place them in a small paper bag, punch air holes in it, and tie it closed with twine, also securing the ends of the sprigs. Set this bag back into the drying space and leave there for another 12 hours or overnight.

3. Remove from the drying space and hang the bag in your kitchen. Shake the bag from time to time to release the herbs from the branch. In a few days, remove the branches from the bag and place the loose herbs in a dry glass container with a lid. Store in a dark place.

### Oven-Roasting

This technique brings out the natural sugars of foods and adds flavor. The fruits and vegetables remain moist during the process.

1. Drizzle the food with olive oil and toss in sea salt; add fresh herbs if desired.

2. Roast at 180° to 200°F for 5 to 6 hours, or at 225° to 250°F for 3 to 4 hours, depending on the food being roasted. Roast fruits and vegetables with higher moisture content or those that are more delicate (such as tomatoes, ripe stone fruits, and citrus) at lower temperatures for a longer time. For sturdier fruits and vegetables or those with lower moisture content (such as root vegetables, pineapple, and apples), roast at higher temperatures for a shorter time.

## Oven-Roasted Nuts

Using a cooling 250°F wood-fired oven, or a grill over indirect heat, toss 4 cups of dry raw nuts in 3 tablespoons olive oil and 2 teaspoons sea salt. Spread the nuts out in a shallow baking dish and roast until the coating is dry and the nuts are fragrant, about 30 minutes, depending on the size and oil content of the nut. Store in an airtight container for up to 3 weeks. You can make other flavored versions by tossing with the juice of 1 lime and a little paprika or cayenne or ground cumin before roasting. Or toss a sprig of rosemary into the dish as you are roasting walnuts, then add a dusting of orange zest as the walnuts cool. Eat as a snack or use as a garnish on salads or chopped to finish fish.

### Spit-Roasting

This method evenly roasts while imparting smoky flavors from the fire. The fruits and vegetables remain moist during the process.

1. Rub the food lightly with olive oil and place in the roasting drum. Suspend the rotisserie basket 8 inches or so from hot coals in a fire pit or grill. Slowly spit-roast until blistered or charred (up to 1 hour) depending on the desired results. Let cool.

2. Portion and store in self-sealing plastic bags, then freeze, or place in a glass container, cover with olive oil, and seal. Store in a cool, dark place.

### Oven-Cooking and Grilling

This is the easiest form of basic food preserving. Cooking and grilling over moderate to high temperatures creates grill and char marks that add flavor to fruits and vegetables, which remain moist during the process.

1. Toss, rub, or brush the fruits or vegetables with olive oil. Lightly salt. Grill-mark over direct heat, then move to indirect heat to finish cooking. For a smokier flavor and less char, plank the vegetables as you would salmon or steak.

2. Let cool before storing in self-sealing plastic bags, or cover with olive oil in an airtight glass container. Refrigerate for up to 1 month.

## Herb-Infused Olive Oil

Using a 3- to 4-inch-deep clay baker, lay clean dry branches or sprigs of herbs in the bottom and cover with 1 inch of olive oil. Place the baker in a preheated 400° to 450°F oven or on a grill over indirect heat and bring to a simmer. Cook for 20 to 25 minutes, then remove from the heat and let cool. Loosely cover with a lid or aluminum foil and leave out overnight for the flavor to develop. Drain and pour the oil into a sterilized glass container and seal. Store in a cool, dark place for up to 6 months. You may add additional ingredients such as dried chiles or peppercorns to the oil, if desired.

## Nuts Toasted in Olive Oil and Nut-Flavored Oil

Using a 3- to 4-inch-deep clay baker, lay clean, dry, skinned and/or cleaned nuts such as almonds, pine nuts, walnuts, or hazelnuts in the bottom and cover by 1/2 inch with olive oil. Place the baker in a 400° to 450°F oven or on a grill over indirect heat and bring to a simmer. Let simmer for 20 to 25 minutes to toast the nuts. Remove from the heat and strain out the nuts, drain them on paper towels, and let the oil cool. Toss the toasted nuts in sea salt, let cool, and place in an airtight container. Strain out any particles and place the oil in a glass container and seal. Store in the refrigerator for up to 2 weeks.

## Meats, Cheeses, and Vegetables

### Smoking

There are two types of smoking processes based on the temperature of the smoke and the desired amount of flavor. The temperature and timeline depend on what type of food is being smoked and what type of smoker is being used. (See below for temperature guidelines.) *Cold smoking* is done at lower temperatures just to add flavor; *hot-smoking* is done at higher temperatures that actually cook the food in addition to adding flavor. Hot-smoking is done above 120°F, typically from 200° to 250°F for meat. Cold-smoking is done at temperatures below those to cook food, generally 70° to 100°F.

---

## Temperature Ranges for Hot-Smoking

**MEATS**
Beef: Brisket, boneless chuck roast: 190° to 225°F
Pork: Tenderloin, shoulder/butt, ribs: 170° to 225°F

**POULTRY**
Chicken, turkey, duck: 165° to 225°F

**FISH**
Salmon, swordfish, halibut, tuna, trout, sardines, whole or cut into fillets or steaks: 150° to 190°F
Note: Oily fish such as salmon or tuna are best for smoking, though most fish can be smoked

**SHELLFISH: 130° TO 150°F**

**VEGETABLES: 225° TO 250°F**
Portobello slices: 200° to 220°F for 15 to 20 minutes
Portobello caps: 200° to 220°F for 25 to 30 minutes
Peppers: 200° to 220°F for 65 to 75 minutes
Garlic head: 200° to 220°F for 25 to 30 minutes
Onion slices: 200° to 225°F for 25 to 30 minutes

---

Curing of some kind occurs prior to cold-smoking. Cold-smoking is preferable for foods that could be damaged by the higher temperature of hot-smoking.

### HOT-SMOKING

Often called smoke cookery, hot-smoking refers to cooking while smoking at 150° to 275°F, depending on the size of the food being smoked. The food being smoked does not require prior brining or curing, though some marinating or a rub is often desirable. Hot-smoking can be done in an oven, a cooker, a smoker, or on a grill over indirect heat and might require a few hours or several days. Low and slow cooking combined with smoke flavors the food and transforms the color and texture. The internal temperature of the meat or fish is important to the safety of the product.

### SMOKING MEAT, POULTRY, AND FISH

Either start a small fire or reserve some coals from a preexisting fire. In an oven, build a single-brick and rack system, as you would for drying or cold-smoking. The rack should be 8 to 10 inches above the embers. Place the embers under the rack. If using a grill, spread out the embers in the bottom. Whether for an oven or a grill, choose a metal pan large enough to span over most of the embers and fill with presoaked oak, maple, or hickory hardwood chips, herbs, or well-dampened hardwood sawdust.

Place the pan directly over the embers. The pan will serve as a barrier between the coals and the food. Put the grill grate in place. Set a perforated pizza pan on the grate. Set the food on the perforated pan over indirect heat. Cover the grill or close the oven door; the oven door should be left slightly open for venting, and the grill vents should be open. Remember, we want low heat and smoke. Cook until the desired internal temperature is achieved and the exterior is golden brown.

## COLD-SMOKING

Smoking food at low temperatures, combined with brining or curing, yields food that is both flavored and preserved. Meat, poultry, fish, or cheese can be smoked using this method, but here we will focus only on cheese because it does not require curing. (Cheese is the exception to the rule; because it is already edible, it does not need to be brined or cured before being cold-smoked.) Refer to the Bibliography for many excellent books covering all smoking options.

## SMOKING CHEESE IN A WOOD-FIRED OVEN, COOKER, OR GRILL

A hard or semi-soft cheese works best as it is solid enough to withstand the process and remain intact.

1. Use a low heat, 100°F or under, to keep from melting the cheese. If you need to cool down the temperature quickly or if the heat is too high in general, add some ice cubes to the pan along with the dampened chips.

2. Reserve some burned-down embers from your fire. In an oven, build a single-brick and rack system as you would for drying. The rack should be 8 to 10 inches above the embers. Place the embers under the rack. If using a grill, spread out the embers in the bottom. Whether using an oven or a grill, choose a metal pan large enough to span over most of the embers and fill with presoaked oak, maple, or hickory hardwood chips, herbs, or well-dampened hardwood sawdust.

3. Place the pan directly over the embers. The pan will serve as a barrier between the heat and the cheese. Put the grill grate in place. Place a tight mesh grate or pizza screen on the grate. Set the cheese on the mesh or screen. Close the oven door or cover the grill; the oven door should be left slightly open for venting, and the grill vents should be open. Closely watch the cheese to make sure it doesn't get too warm. The temperature is correct if fat comes to the surface of the cheese. Smoke the cheese until the exterior is golden brown. Wipe off any surface fat.

4. To store, let cool, cover, and refrigerate.

## Using Aromatics

The choice of aromatic woods for smoking is based on what's being smoked and the desired flavor of the smoking ingredients. Refer to the "Cooking Hardwoods and Fruitwoods Chart," page 11, for the commonly used hardwoods for cooking. Chips, chunks, and sawdust of these same hardwoods are commonly used for smoking. Sawdust should be damp, chips should be soaked for 30 minutes, and chunks for at least 1 hour before using.

### OTHER AROMATICS

Other aromatics to throw on the hot coals include grapevine cuttings, olive branches, fennel branches, nut shells or cracked whole nuts, olive and fruit pits, fresh herbs, dried herb cuttings, dried bay leaves, citrus peels, juniper berries, star anise clusters, whole nutmegs, teas, tobacco, and coffee beans. Soak all aromatics for at least 30 minutes prior to use or use green to create smoke.

## Smoked, Flavored, and Wood-Roasted Sea Salts

Smoked sea salts add a burst of flavor to raw and cooked foods when used as finishing or condiment salts. The options and flavors you can create are limitless. Anything from the aromatics list (opposite) will impart magical flavor to pure sea salt. Take it a step further and add other flavorings by tossing them into the salt before smoking.

MAKES 1 CUP

1 cup coarse sea salt
1 to 2 teaspoons flavoring ingredient

To smoke, mix the salt and 1 teaspoon of the flavoring ingredient together and spread on a baking sheet or in a baking dish. Place in a 175°F (or lower) closed wood-fired oven or grill for 3 to 4 hours. Let cool.

If you want less smokiness, smoke only the sea salt, then add the other flavoring after. For more intense citrus flavor, add a few drops of citrus oil to the jar and shake to distribute.

To flavor, mix the salt and 2 teaspoons of flavoring ingredient (such as peppercorns, citrus zest, lavender, vanilla bean, nutmeg, smoky paprika, or crumbled tomato skin from oven-roasted tomatoes) together and add to a glass jar.

To roast, spread the salt in a small cast-iron skillet or clay baking dish. Moisten evenly with water or a flavored liquid such as tea, coffee, or even mushroom liquid. If using just water, add a powdered flavoring such as green tea or powdered mushrooms to the moistened salt. Slowly roast in a wood-fired oven, cooker or covered grill until the salt dries. Let cool.

Store flavored salt in an airtight glass container in a cool, dark place.

## Oven-Roasted Tomatoes

MAKES 6 TO 8 CUPS

4 pounds small plum or pear-shaped tomatoes
    such as Roma
Olive oil, for drizzling
Kosher salt

Prepare a medium heat fire (325°F) in a wood-fired oven. Cut tomatoes in half lengthwise and remove the seeds. Drizzle with olive oil, lightly salt, and toss.

Place, cut side up, on baking sheets lined with parchment paper. Bake in the oven until the skin is wrinkled and juices have been mostly absorbed but the flesh is still moist and soft, 1 to 2 hours. Remove from the oven and let cool. Pack in an airtight container and store in a cool, dark place. Reserve any juices to use in sauces.

NOTE

If the skins are not to be used in the dish, roast the tomatoes cut side down and remove skins after the tomatoes are slightly cooled. If you want the charred flavor of the tomato in the dish, roast cut side down and leave the skins on after roasting.

# Smoky Romesco Sauce

MAKES ABOUT 4 CUPS

3 ripe tomatoes, cut in half crosswise

1 yellow onion, cut in half lengthwise

1 head of garlic

Olive oil, for drizzling

3/4 cup piquillo peppers, chopped

1/2 cup sliced almonds, toasted

1/2 cup hazelnuts, toasted, skinned, and chopped

1 slice day-old bread, torn

1 cup olive oil

1 ancho chile, toasted, seeded, and chopped

1 to 2 tablespoons sweet pimentón (Spanish smoked paprika)

1/4 teaspoon red pepper flakes (optional)

1/4 cup or more sherry vinegar

Kosher salt

Prepare a medium-hot fire (400°F) in a wood-fired oven, cooker, or grill.

Place the tomatoes and onion, cut side down, on a parchment-lined baking sheet. Using a large knife, cut the top 3/4 inch off the head of garlic and place the head on the baking sheet, cut side up. Drizzle with olive oil and roast in an oven or cooker, or cook over direct heat on a grill until the skins of the tomatoes are wrinkled and charred and the onions are slightly soft, 20 to 30 minutes.

Remove the skins from the tomatoes and onion and coarsely chop the flesh. Place in a food processor along with any juice from the roasting. Squeeze the roasted garlic from 5 large cloves into the mixture. Add the piquillo peppers and pulse to chop. Add the nuts and torn bread. With the machine running, drizzle in one-third of the olive oil. Add the ancho, pimentón, red pepper flakes, and half of the sherry vinegar. Increase the speed to incorporate the ingredients and chop the nuts. Add salt to taste. Add more olive oil and continue to process until the desired texture is reached. Add water if too thick. Adjust the taste by adding more sherry vinegar and olive oil if needed.

# Roasted Corn and Smoky Tomato Salsa

MAKES ABOUT 3 1/2 CUPS

1/4 cup plus 2 tablespoons olive oil

Kernels from 2 ears of corn

2 cups mixed cherry tomatoes, halved

1 dried ancho chile

4 cloves toasted garlic (page 192), skins removed

1 teaspoon sweet pimentón (Spanish smoked paprika)

Zest and juice of 1 lime

Kosher salt

Prepare a medium-heat fire (375°F) in a wood-fired oven or cooker.

In a small bowl, toss the corn kernels in 1 tablespoon of olive oil. Line a sheet pan with parchment paper, then spread the kernels on the pan.

In a second small bowl, toss the tomatoes in 1 tablespoon of olive oil to coat, then lightly salt. Line a second sheet pan with parchment paper, then place the tomatoes cut-side down on the pan.

Rehydrate the chile by placing it in a bowl with warm water for 30 minutes, making sure it is fully submerged. Slice the garlic cloves into thin slivers.

Place both sheet pans in the oven and roast for 10 to 12 minutes, until the corn is golden. Remove the corn, and continue roasting the tomatoes for 10 more minutes, until they are shriveled and soft. Remove the tomatoes and set aside.

Transfer the roasted corn, tomatoes, and any juices to a bowl. Using a small knife, remove the stem from the chile, then slice it lengthwise and scrape out the seeds. Finely chop the chile, then add it to the corn and tomatoes along with the garlic and pimentón. Mix until well combined. Add the lime zest and juice, olive oil, and salt to taste.

Set aside for 20 to 30 minutes before serving, to allow flavors to blend. Use now, or cover and refrigerate for up to 1 week. Serve at room temperature.

# Smoky Eggplant Caponata with Toasted Pine Nuts

Caponata is a classic appetizer spread that has the sweet and sour balanced components of many Mediterranean dishes. Here, the eggplant, red pepper, and onions are cooked in the wood-fired oven before being combined with salty capers and toasted pine nuts. It can be added to a pasta salad or used as the filling in an omelet or frittata.

MAKES ABOUT 3 CUPS

1 globe eggplant, cut into 1/2-inch cubes

Kosher salt

Olive oil, for cooking

1 large yellow onion, cut into small dice

2 stalks celery, cut into small dice

1 red bell pepper, roasted, peeled, and diced, (see page 191)

1/2 cup oil-cured black olives, pitted and coarsely chopped

2 tablespoons capers, drained

2 cloves roasted garlic (see page 192), thinly sliced

3/4 cup diced fresh or canned tomatoes

1/3 cup red wine vinegar

1 1/2 tablespoons sugar

Freshly ground black pepper

2 tablespoons pine nuts, toasted in olive oil, toasted oil reserved (see page 184)

Prepare a hot fire (400°F) in a wood-fired oven or grill.

Place the eggplant in a colander and sprinkle with salt. Let drain over the sink or a bowl for 30 to 40 minutes. Rinse under cold water and pat dry with paper towels. Set aside.

Pour 1/2 inch of olive oil into a large cast-iron skillet and heat it in the oven until hot enough to make a piece of eggplant sizzle. Add the eggplant and roast in the oven until golden, about 10 minutes. Using a slotted spoon, transfer to paper towels to drain, then transfer to a bowl.

In the same pan, heat the reserved olive oil from the toasted pine nuts and roast the onion until translucent, about 10 minutes. Remove with a slotted spoon and add to the eggplant. Reheat the oil and sauté the celery for 4 to 5 minutes. Remove and add to the eggplant mixture. Add the bell pepper, olives, capers, and sliced garlic to the eggplant mixture.

Heat the tomatoes in the skillet in the oven until they come to a simmer, then add the vinegar, sugar, and black pepper to taste. Simmer for another 5 minutes to dissolve the sugar. Remove from the heat, add the toasted pine nuts, and add to the bowl of vegetables. Mix well. Taste and adjust the seasoning. Let cool to room temperature and serve, or cover and refrigerate for up to 2 days. Bring to room temperature before serving.

# Grilled Fruit Chutney

In India, chutneys are used as condiments to accompany curries. In our culture, they can be used to brighten up any number of roasted or grilled meats or fish. This version is grilled over a wood fire. Chutney can be made from a variety of fruits combined with raisins, an acid such as vinegar or juice, ginger, and some traditional Indian spices to create a fabulous condiment. Its flavors will continue to develop during storage.

MAKES ABOUT 4 CUPS

4 firm apricots, halved and pitted

1 pineapple, peeled, cored, and cut into 1/2-inch slices

1 teaspoon grated fresh ginger

3 tablespoons golden raisins

1/4 teaspoon yellow or brown mustard seeds

1/4 teaspoon ground turmeric (optional)

Grated zest and juice of 1 large orange

11/2 tablespoons light brown sugar

1/2 teaspoon cayenne pepper

1/2 teaspoon kosher salt

Prepare a wood-fired grill for cooking with indirect heat.

Grill the fruit on both sides until well marked, about 3 minutes each side. Remove and let cool, then cut into chunks. Combine all of the remaining ingredients, then toss with the grilled fruit and place in a baking dish. Place the dish over indirect heat on the grill and cook for 15 minutes to heat through and let flavors combine. Remove from the heat and let cool. Cover and refrigerate overnight, or up to 2 weeks. Bring to room temperature before using.

# Warm Olives with Fennel and Orange

These smoky flavored olives are always the first thing to disappear off an antipasti platter or hors d'oeuvres spread. The brightness of the orange zest enhances the earthy flavors of the olives; you can use freshly squeezed orange juice if you don't have zest. I love to serve these straight from the oven, still warm.

MAKES ABOUT 21/2 CUPS

1 cup picholine olives with pits

1 cup niçoise olives with pits

1/2 cup oil-cured black olives with pits

1/4 cup olive oil

2 tablespoons minced fresh thyme

2 cloves garlic, minced

1 tablespoon fennel seeds, bruised

Strips of orange zest from 1 orange

1 tablespoon white wine vinegar

Prepare a hot fire (400°F) in a wood-fired oven, cooker, or grill.

Soak the picholine and niçoise olives in water to cover for 10 minutes, then drain. Combine the drained olives, oil-cured olives, oil, thyme, garlic, fennel seeds, and orange zest in a baking dish and roast uncovered until the garlic is fragrant and the olives are hot, about 10 minutes. Remove from the heat and add the vinegar. Toss to combine. Let cool slightly, then serve warm. To store, cover and refrigerate for up to 1 month. The flavor gets better with time. Rewarm to serve.

# Wood-Roasted Red Pepper Wine Sauce

This simple sauce has many applications: as a sauce for meat (page 54), as a pasta sauce, or as a soup base. Wood-roasting the peppers and onions adds great flavor. Returning them to the fire along with the wine and other ingredients adds a richness and depth to the sauce. Use a red wine that has a lot of presence such as Zinfandel or Sangiovese. You can add other spices, such as a curry blend or chipotles in adobo, as you choose.

MAKES ABOUT 2 CUPS

2 large red bell peppers

1 yellow onion, halved

3 cloves roasted garlic (see page 192)

1/4 cup olive oil

1 cup dry red wine

1/2 teaspoon dried herbs of choice

2 teaspoons honey

Kosher salt and freshly ground white pepper

Pinch of red pepper flakes (optional)

Place the bell peppers in the embers of a wood-fired oven or over the direct heat of a grill. Roast until well blistered and charred all over. Place in a bowl, covered with plastic wrap, and let stand for 10 minutes. Remove the skin, seeds, and stem. Reserve any juice. Cut into chunks. Roast the onion, cut side down on the grill or skin side down in the embers, until slightly caramelized. Remove the skin and coarsely chop.

Combine the peppers, reserved juice, onion, garlic, olive oil, wine, and herbs in a baking dish and place on the floor of the wood-fired oven or over indirect heat on the grill. Cook, uncovered, until liquid is slightly reduced, 10 to 15 minutes. Remove from the heat and let cool. Place

in a blender or food processor and puree. Strain through a fine-mesh sieve, pushing down on the solids with the back of a large spoon. Season with the honey and salt and pepper to taste. Add the pepper flakes, if you like. Thin with a touch of warm water or vegetable stock if needed. Use warm, or store in portions in self-sealing plastic bags in the refrigerator for 1 week or in your freezer for up to 2 months.

# Roasted Lemon-Shallot Vinaigrette

Roasting lemons and shallots brings out their natural sugars and imparts a smoky flavor as well. Try variations, too, such as oranges and large cloves of garlic.

MAKES ABOUT 3 1/2 CUPS

4 lemons, scrubbed, each cut into 4 wedges

4 unpeeled large shallots, halved lengthwise

Olive oil, for drizzling

1/2 teaspoon kosher salt

1 bay leaf (optional)

Prepare a medium heat fire (350°F) in a wood-fired oven or cooker.

Place the lemons and shallots, cut side down, in a clay baking dish. Season with a drizzle of olive oil and the salt, add the bay leaf, and roast until the shallots and lemons are tender, about 25 minutes. Remove from the oven and let cool. Remove the bay leaf, peel the shallots, and then coarsely chop the shallots and lemon wedges. Place the entire contents of the dish, including the roasting liquid, into an airtight container and refrigerate. The next day, divide into 1/2-cup amounts, seal in airtight containers, and refrigerate for up to 3 weeks.

# Green Olive Tapenade

MAKES ABOUT 4 CUPS

½ red onion, coarsely chopped

¼ cup unseasoned rice vinegar

8 ounces green olives (in brine), rinsed, pitted, and minced

1 fennel bulb, finely chopped

1 tablespoon salted capers, rinsed and dried

3 cloves roasted garlic, minced

½ cup Italian parsley leaves, minced

2 anchovy fillets, finely minced (optional)

½ cup olive oil

2 small oranges, peeled, sectioned, and cut into chunks

2 tablespoons orange zest

2 tablespoons orange juice

Kosher salt

Finely ground white pepper

To make a chunky tapenade, in a small bowl, toss the onion in the rice vinegar until coated and set aside. In a medium bowl, combine the olives, fennel, capers, and garlic. Add the parsley, anchovy, ¼ cup of the olive oil, and the orange chunks, zest, and juice. Drain the onion and combine with the olive mixture. Add the remaining ¼ cup of olive oil and season with white pepper to taste.

To make a smooth tapenade, in a food processor, blend all of the ingredients together to the desired consistency.

Transfer to a bowl. Set the tapenade aside for at least 30 minutes before serving, to allow flavors to blend. Use now, or cover and refrigerate for up to 1 week.

# Garlic: Blanched, Poached, Roasted, or Toasted

Garlic can be enhanced in a number of ways, each having their own flavor profile. Blanching in water prevents oxidation (and therefore harshness). Poaching in olive oil does the same thing, and yields garlic-flavored olive oil that can be used for basting, coating, and vinaigrettes. Roasted garlic can be sliced as cloves or mashed into a luscious puree that will melt into sauces. Toasting garlic gives it a nutty flavor that is all its own.

**Blanching:** Bring a small saucepan of water to a low boil. Separate the cloves from 1 head of garlic, leaving the skins on, and drop into water for 5 minutes. Remove and drain. Store, skin on, in an airtight container in the refrigerator for up to 1 week.

**Poaching:** In a small cast-iron pot, bring 1 cup olive oil to a very low simmer on a grill or in a wood-fired oven and drop peeled cloves from 1 head of garlic in to cook for 10 minutes. Remove, drain, let cool, and store in an airtight container in the refrigerator for up to 1 week. Reserve the poaching oil and use as a flavoring or finishing oil.

**Roasting:** Garlic is easy to roast and develops much more flavor in a wood-fired environment. Simply cut the top off a whole head of garlic to expose the cloves and drizzle with a bit of olive oil. Place in a small clay cooker or cast-iron pot or an aluminum-foil packet and place in the wood-fired oven or on a covered grill to roast until soft to the touch, about 20 minutes. Store in an airtight container in the refrigerator for up to 2 weeks.

**Toasting:** Toast the skin-on cloves from 1 head of garlic in a dry skillet over high heat until the skins are slightly browned. You are *toasting* but not *cooking* the garlic. Slice or mince the garlic as called for in the recipe. Store in an airtight container and refrigerate for up to 2 weeks.

# RESOURCES

Here's a list of some of my favorite suppliers for wood-fired cooking.

## Wood-Fired Appliances

Aztec Grill
www.aztecgrill.com
Professional-quality wood-fired grills.

Forno Bravo
www.fornobravo.com
Italian refractory ovens.

Heartland Appliances
www.heartlandapp.com
Artisan wood-fired stoves.

La Caja China
www.lacajachina.com
Cuban Box roaster.

Mugnaini
www.mugnaini.com
Italian refractory ovens.

NapaStyle
www.napastyle.com
Beehive ovens, Florentine grills, Tuscan grills.

Ovencrafters
www.ovencrafters.net
Masonry oven builders.

Pacific Coast Brick Ovens
www.pcbrickovens.com
Wood-fired and dual-fired ovens made domestically.

Pitts & Spitts
www.pittsandspitts.com
Smokers.

SoJoe Fire Pits
www.sojoe.com
Fire pits and rotisseries.

The Big Green Egg
www.biggreenegg.com
Ceramic cooker-smoker.

Vesta Fire Ovens
www.vestafireusa.com
Portable fire brick ovens.

Wood Stone Ovens
www.woodstone-corp.com
Wood-fired and dual-fuel ovens and tandoors.

## Cookware

Bill Sax Flameware Pottery
413-532-4236

Berber Trading
www.tagines.com or www.berbertrading.com
Tagines.

Felipe Ortega
www.felipeortega.com
Custom Native American micaceous pottery.

Forno Bravo
www.fornobravo.com/terracotta-bakeware
Italian terra-cotta cookware.

## Cookware, *continued*

Gourmet Sleuth
www.gourmetsleuth.com
Mexican and La Chamba clay cookware.

Italian Kitchen
www.italiankitchen.com
Mario Batali cookware, piastra granite griddle.

La Cuisine
www.lacuisine.com
Piral Italian clay cookware.

L'Atelier Vert
www.frenchgardening.com
French clay cookware.

La Tienda
www.tienda.com
Spanish cookware.

Lodge Manufacturing
www.lodgemfg.com
Cast-iron cookware.

Pacific Rim Gourmet
www.pacificrim-gourmet.com
Asian clay pots.

Romertopf Clay Bakers
www.claypot.com
German clay cookware.

Spitjack
www.spitjack.com
Cast-iron "spyder" skillets.

The Spanish Table
www.spanishtable.com
Cazuelas, paella pans.

Toque Blanche
www.mytoque.com
La Chamba clay, Emil Henri cookware.

Villa Paradiso
www.villaparadisohome.com
Italian terra-cotta bakeware.

## Tools & Accessories

Coffee Roasters
www.coffeeroastersclub.com
Rotisserie drum baskets.

Forno Bravo
www.fornobravo.com
Pizza oven tools and grates.

Italian Kitchen
www.italiankitchen.com
Mario Batali's piastra granite griddle.

NapaStyle
www.napastyle.com
Tuscan grill, grilling accessories.

SoJoe Fire Pits
www.sojoe.com
Rotisseries.

Spitjack
www.spitjack.com
Rotisseries.

Wood Stone Ovens
www.woodstone-corp.com
Pizza oven tools.

## Regional Hardwood & Charcoal

To reduce the carbon footprint on your hardwood or lump charcoal purchase, try to buy from local sources. Here are selected regional sources.

Apple Creek Timber (Washington)
www.applecreektimberinc.com

BBQWoods (Washington)
www.barbecuewood.com

Cowboy Charcoal (Tennessee)
www.cowboycharcoal.com

Gourmet Wood Products (Texas)
www.gourmetwood.com

Lazzari Charcoal (California)
www.lazzari.com

Nature's Own (Rhode Island)
www.char-wood.com

Paul Bunyan's Firewood (Arizona)
www.paulbunyansfirewood.com

Wicked Good Charcoal (Maine)
www.wickedgoodcharcoal.com

## Grilling & Roasting Planks

Fire & Flavor Grilling Co.
www.fireandflavor.com
Aromatic grilling planks and papers.

Nature's Cuisine
www.natures-cuisine.com
Aromatic grilling and roasting planks.

## Food Products

Adriana's Caravan
www.adrianascaravan.com
Herbs and spices.

Anson Mills
www.ansonmills.com
Heirloom corn, wheat, and rice.

Artisan Foie Gras
www.artisanfoiegras.com
Artisan duck products.

Formaggio Kitchen
www.formaggiokitchen.com
Cheeses, olive oils, pastas.

Heritage Foods, USA
www.heritagefoodusa.com
Turkeys and meats.

La Quercia
www.laquercia.us
Artisan cured meats.

Penzey's
www.penzeys.com
Spices.

Purcell Mountain Farms
www.purcellmountainfarms.com
Lentils and grains.

Rancho Gordo Beans
www.ranchogordo.com
Dried heirloom beans.

The Olive Press
www.theolivepress.com
Artisan olive oils and olive products.

## Classes, Camps, and Tutorials

To learn more about wood-fired cooking through classes and instructional hands-on experience, I recommend the following resources. Check my website, www.elementsoftaste.com, for updates to this list.

Elements of Taste
www.elementsoftaste.com
My website, which lists current and upcoming class offerings.

Culinary Institute of America at Greystone
www.ciachef.edu/california/enthusiasts
Sophisticated Palate program.

John Ash
www.chefjohnash.com
Voted Cooking Teacher of the Year 2008, John Ash is the chair of the Sophisticated Palate Program at the CIA, Greystone.

Ramekins Cooking School, Sonoma
www.ramekins.com

Mary Karlin's Live Fire Cooking Camps
www.livefirecookingcamp.com
Offered in select locations across the United States.

La Cocina Que Canta Culinary Center
www.lacocinaquecanta.com
Located at Rancho La Puerta, Baja California, Mexico.

# BIBLIOGRAPHY

Ackerman, Diane. *A Natural History of The Senses*. New York: Vintage Books, 1991.

Aidells, Bruce. *Bruce Aidell's Complete Book of Pork*. New York: William Morrow, 2004.

Algar, Ayla. *Classical Turkish Cooking: Traditional Turkish Food for the American Kitchen*. New York: Harper-Collins Publishers, 1991.

Beard, James A. and Helen Evans Brown. *The Complete Book of Outdoor Cookery*. New York: Marlowe & Company, 1983.

Brennan, Georgeanne. *The Mediterranean Herb Cookbook: Fresh and Savory Recipes from the Mediterranean Garden*. San Francisco: Chronicle Books, 2000.

Cardoz, Floyd. *One Spice, Two Spice*. New York: Harper-Collins Publishers, 2006.

Carroll, Ricki. *Home Cheese Making*. North Adams, Mass.: Storey Publishing, 2002.

Dubbs, Chris and Dave Heberle. *Smoking Food*. New York: Skyhorse Publishing, 2008.

Goldstein, Joyce. *Italian Slow and Savory*. San Francisco: Chronicle Books, 2004.

Guillen, Dina, et al. *The Plank Grilling Cookbook*. Seattle: Sasquatch Books, 2006.

Helou, Anissa. *Mediterranean Street Food*. New York: William Morrow, 2002.

Jamison, Cheryl Alters and Bill. *Sublime Smoke*. Boston: Harvard Common Press, 1996.

————. *Smoke & Spice*. Boston: Harvard Common Press, Revised 2003.

Madison, Deborah. *Vegetarian Suppers from Deborah Madison's Kitchen*. New York: Broadway Books, 2005.

McGee, Harold. *On Food & Cooking*. New York: Scribner, 2004.

Perkins, Wilma Lord. *The New Fannie Farmer Boston Cooking School Cook Book*. Boston: Little, Brown and Company, Ninth Edition, 1951.

Peterson, James. *Vegetables*. New York: William Morrow, 1998.

Rombauer, Irma S. *The Joy of Cooking*. New York: Scribner, 2006 Edition.

Rubel, William. *The Magic of Fire: Hearth Cooking*. Berkeley, Calif.: Ten Speed Press, 2002.

Ruhlman, Michael, and Brian Polcyn. *Charcuterie*. New York: W. W. Norton & Company, 2005.

Sandler, Nick, and Johnny Acton. *Preserved*. London: Kyle Books, 2004.

Schulz, Phillip Stephen. *Cooking with Fire & Smoke*. New York: Fireside Books, 1986.

Scott, Alan, and Daniel Wing. *The Bread Builders: Hearth Loaves and Masonry Ovens*. White River, Vermont: Chelsea Green Publishing, 1999.

Stevens, Molly. *All About Braising*. New York: W. W. Norton & Company, 2004.

The Browns. *America Cooks: Favorite Recipes from 48 States*. New York: Halcyon House, 1949.

Thomas, Dian. *Roughing It Easy*. Holladay, Utah: Dian Thomas Publishing Company, 1994.

Waters, Alice. *The Art of Simple Food*. New York: Clarkson Potter, 2007.

Wolfert, Paula. *The Slow Mediterranean Kitchen*. New York: John Wiley & Sons, 2003.

Yotnegparian, Maurice Sabbagh. *Cooking with Fire*. Glendale, Calif.: Earthstone Woodfire Ovens, 2007.

# INDEX